T0294342

HOLIDAY SEASONS

AUP STUDIES IN CULTURAL AND SOCIAL HISTORY, 4
SERIES EDITORS: CAROLINE DALEY AND DEBORAH MONTGOMERIE

Holiday Seasons

CHRISTMAS, NEW YEAR AND EASTER IN
NINETEENTH-CENTURY NEW ZEALAND

ALISON CLARKE

AUCKLAND UNIVERSITY PRESS

First published 2007

Auckland University Press
University of Auckland
Private Bag 92019
Auckland, New Zealand
www.auckland.ac.nz/aup

ISBN-13: 978 1 86940 382 9
ISSN 1176-9882

National Library of New Zealand Cataloguing-in-Publication Data
Clarke, Alison (Alison Jane), 1962-
Holiday seasons : Christmas, New Year and Easter in
nineteenth-century New Zealand / Alison Clarke.
(AUP studies in cultural and social history, 1176-9882 ; 4)
Includes bibliographical references and index.
ISBN 978-1-86940-382-9
1. Holidays—New Zealand—History—19th century.
2. Festivals—New Zealand—History—19th century.
I. Title. II. Series.
394.26—dc 22

COVER DESIGN: Base Two
FRONT COVER IMAGE: A picnic near New Plymouth.
F-28204-1/2, CROMPTON-SMITH COLLECTION, ALEXANDER TURNBULL LIBRARY, WELLINGTON.
BACK COVER IMAGES: Father Francois Melu and altar boys at St Mary's Catholic Church, Otaki, at Easter 1884
and The Westland family at their campsite, probably near Arthur's Pass, over Christmas and New Year of 1894–95.
MARIST ARCHIVES, WELLINGTON AND CP 8410, 135-5&7, WESTLAND FAMILY ALBUM, A. C. GRAHAM COLLECTION,
MACMILLAN BROWN LIBRARY, UNIVERSITY OF CANTERBURY.

Printed by Printlink Ltd, Wellington

CONTENTS

AUP STUDIES IN CULTURAL AND SOCIAL HISTORY

Edited by Caroline Daley and Deborah Montgomerie, this series
is a forum for rethinking key aspects of New Zealand's past in a lively
and accessible way. Generously illustrated and extensively researched,
the books capture the mood of times past while also asking why
New Zealand history matters and how it should be written.

ALSO IN THE SERIES
1. *Love in Time of War: Letter Writing in the Second World War*,
Deborah Montgomerie
2. *Going Up, Going Down: The Rise and Fall of the Department Store*,
Helen B. Laurenson
3. *The Bookmen's Dominion: Cultural Life in New Zealand 1920–1950*,
Chris Hilliard

ACKNOWLEDGEMENTS

Researching and writing about holidays has been an enjoyable project, and many people have helped make the task a pleasurable one. First and foremost, I am grateful to the series editors, Caroline Daley and Deborah Montgomerie, for encouraging the book project in the first place and then making wise suggestions which greatly improved the initial manuscript. Elizabeth Caffin and the Auckland University Press staff have also been most encouraging and helpful: thank you to Katrina Duncan, Christine O'Brien, Annie Irving and fabulous editor Anna Hodge.

I first started researching holidays some years ago for my PhD thesis. This book includes some of the material used in that thesis, but has been written from scratch and incorporates new material from beyond the initial regional focus of the dissertation. The staff of the Department of History, University of Otago, were greatly supportive during my student days and in the years since, and nobody could ask for a better supervisor and mentor than John Stenhouse. I am also grateful to the postgraduate students who made me a better writer by pulling my work to bits and allowing me to practise my editing skills on their work in return: thank you James Beattie and the notorious 'reading group' of David Clark, Meredith Gibb, Richard Lummis, Lachy Paterson, Bobbi Schijf and Tim Thomas. When I presented a paper on New Year at the 'Scots Abroad' conference at the Stout Research Centre, Victoria University of Wellington, in July 2006, several people made helpful comments and Ewen Grant and Brad Patterson provided useful references, for which I am most grateful.

Many archivists and librarians have contributed to this book. Much of the research was carried out at those two marvellous treasure houses, the Hocken Collections (Dunedin) and the Alexander Turnbull Library (Wellington). To my colleagues at the Hocken and the staff of the Turnbull I am hugely grateful. Special thanks to Hocken Librarian Stuart Strachan, who always took an interest in the project. It is also a pleasure to thank the invariably helpful staff of other institutions who helped with archival or pictorial research for this book: my thanks to those at the Auckland City Libraries Special Collections, Auckland War Memorial Museum, Canterbury Museum, Catholic Archdiocesan Archives (Wellington), Christchurch City Libraries, Lakes District

Museum (Arrowtown), Macmillan Brown Library (University of Canterbury), Marist Archives (Wellington), Methodist Archives (Christchurch), Otago Settlers Museum, Presbyterian Church Archives (Dunedin) and Puke Ariki (New Plymouth). I am grateful to the *New Zealand Herald* / APN for allowing publication of images from the *Weekly News*, and to Veronica Vick for supplying information about the Cowling family.

Thanks also go to the friends and colleagues who have encouraged and supported me while I worked on this book, especially Chris Brickell and Vivien Pullar, who know the joys and frustrations of writing! Last, but most certainly not least, I acknowledge the love and support of my family, who have been wonderfully encouraging throughout this project. My mother, Sheila Clarke, and sister Kathy Clarke kindly acted as representatives of the proverbial 'general reader' and made wise comments on early drafts. I dedicate this book to them, to Irene Clarke and to the memory of Ross Clarke, Ian and Alexa Fraser and many happy family holidays.

⌖

Seasonal Celebrations and
the Making of New Zealand Culture

'I never did enjoy a Christmas since I left home', Charles Hayward declared on Christmas Day 1865, by now a veteran of five New Zealand summers. 'There always seems to be something wanting that one is sure to get in the old country, in fact I may say if one wants to have the full enjoyment of Christmas day, there is only one place I believe in the whole world, and that place I need scarcely say is England.' A reader can almost hear the sighs punctuating his diary entry. Such homesickness can be found in the writings of numerous English migrants to New Zealand. Some revelled in the new opportunities offered by a southern Christmas. Others simply felt miserable. Clearly, Christmas was a very different festival in the colony than at 'home'.

For Hayward, as for many others, the physical environment of his new home – particularly the change of seasons – presented a challenge to familiar Christmas traditions. But just as important was Hayward's new social and cultural environment. A coastal shipping captain, he had married Agnes Lees of the Catlins, South Otago, settling there among the Lees family. The Lees hailed from the Scottish Borders and, along with their neighbours, did not celebrate Christmas. Instead of enjoying the familiar Christmas holiday, Suffolk-born Hayward found himself indulging in the unfamiliar traditions of a Scottish-style New Year a week later, joining his brother-in-law to 'first foot' around the district.[1]

Hayward's experience reminds us that cultural encounter in nineteenth-century New Zealand was not confined to meetings between Maori and Pakeha. Migrants to New Zealand, the majority from Britain and Ireland, brought with them a variety of regional and religious cultures rather than a simple overarching British culture. Sociologist Eviatar Zerubavel has shown that the holiday calendar is powerful in forming communities. Sharing feasts and fasts together promotes group solidarity and defines insiders and outsiders. The classic example of this is the different weekly holy days – Friday, Saturday and Sunday – kept by Muslims, Jews and Christians.[2] New Zealand colonists had many things in common and they shared, with few exceptions, the pattern of the Christian seven-day week. But their traditions and customs also varied, and one major point of cultural difference lay in the holidays they kept. Even if migrants from different backgrounds shared holidays, they did not always celebrate them in similar ways. Thrown together in new communities they encountered these differences and had to adapt.

Holidays were a potent indication of what it meant to be a colonist: a cultural amalgam of old world and new, of north and south, of nostalgia and novelty, of past and future. For Maori, the European holidays were entirely foreign, adopted and adapted into their culture along with another more significant import, the Christian religion. Europeans had little interest in Maori ways of marking time: they introduced their own calendar as part of the colonising process. But Europeans were not all alike, meaning that for Pakeha, too, there were new holidays in the colony. Those of Scottish heritage adopted Christmas and Easter, and those from England and Ireland the new holiday of New Year; these changes came to New Zealand several generations before the three holidays became widespread throughout Britain and Ireland. The Australian colonies followed a similar path to New Zealand, although with differences reflecting their distinctive mix of cultures: St Patrick's Day was far more important in Australia; while New Year was eclipsed by Christmas and never became the two-day holiday enjoyed on this side of the Tasman.[3]

Exploring holidays gives new insights into some of the livelier occasions of nineteenth-century life. These were days which formed highlights in what could be a difficult existence. Holidays also take us to the heart of the development of a new and distinctive New Zealand culture – a sometimes uneasy blend of cherished traditions from elsewhere and customs developed from the local environment. The nineteenth century is the critical period for examining this development. Although a minority who lived in isolation or in small communities without a mixture of ethnicities could continue in their old ways, by the end of the century most New Zealand residents accepted the blend of holiday traditions we now take for granted. The new holidays of the twentieth century – Anzac Day and Waitangi Day – were local creations and have a more 'nationalist' flavour. But the development of New Zealand culture was not simply a matter of the development of national identity; it was far more complex than that. Nineteenth-century residents identified themselves by their family and if Maori their hapu; they also identified as members of a local community, region, religion or ethnic group as much as they saw themselves as 'New Zealanders'. Their membership of the British Empire added another important level of belonging. These elements all contributed to the complex amalgam which would become our culture; the holidays examined in this book reveal some of those complexities.

Why Christmas, New Year and Easter? These holidays remain our major festive occasions in the twenty-first century, and that alone makes them worthy of study, but there are other reasons to investigate them further. Although not recognised by all nineteenth-century residents of New Zealand, they were more widely kept than other holidays, with the possible exception of celebrations of the monarchy. Other festive occasions tended to be of more localised importance, such as the provincial anniversary days, or St Patrick's Day celebrations in Irish communities, or the holidays surrounding Presbyterian communion seasons in the south of the country; Labour Day emerged in the later nineteenth century and was largely an urban event.[4] Christmas, New Year and Easter, however, arrived with the earliest European settlers, and the evolution and spread of these imported holidays over the decades prior to 1900 reveal something of the cultural change colonisation brought to these islands. These festivals have an added intrigue because they were neither purely religious nor purely secular. They were a lively mixture of pious and less pious activities, typical of life in the nineteenth century when spiritual elements were never far below the surface. Investigating the holiday exploits of our forebears provides an insight into a religious world quite unfamiliar to many twenty-first-century New Zealanders, citizens of a more secular age.

Historians have paid plenty of attention to Anzac Day – said by some New Zealanders to mark the birth of our nationhood – but little to our older holidays.[5] Beyond these shores, the holidays (especially Christmas) have attracted far greater interest from scholars. Some historians suggest that many holiday traditions were 'invented' in the nineteenth century; others argue that 'traditions' are always changing, and we can see their evolution over a much longer period. Scholars do agree, however, that holidays are excellent indicators of change in societies and cultures, and some go so far as to suggest that holidays can themselves bring about such change. Historians have used holidays to explore a variety of themes, including family relationships, gender roles, social class, consumer culture, religion and imperialism.[6]

All of these themes have value, but this book is most interested in the way a variety of holiday practices were imported into the place which became New Zealand, and how they evolved in this specific geographic, social and cultural environment. In doing so, it contributes to the growing body of work on ethnic difference within colonial society. As James Belich has pointed out, cultural difference within the Pakeha community was once minimised, reduced, concealed and denied.[7] Recent decades have witnessed increasing interest in the divergent groups which made up the 'British' or 'European' population of New Zealand, generally through the study of specific migrant groups, such as the Irish, the Scots and the Germans. In examining a specific cultural practice – the holiday – rather than a specific ethnic group, this study reveals something of the diverse cultural and religious influences in nineteenth-century New Zealand and the way people from those different traditions influenced one another.

Folklorists have a habit of seeking out ancient and pagan origins for almost every holiday custom. In some cases they are correct. It is clearly not coincidence that the celebration of Christmas and New Year took place, in the northern hemisphere at least, around the time of the winter solstice. Christians did not mark the birth of Jesus with festivities until several generations after his death. Since AD 274, Romans had been celebrating the birth of the sun, the Sol Invictus, on 25 December. When Christians began celebrating Christmas some decades later, they deliberately selected the same date. As Christianity became the official religion of the Roman Empire in the fourth century AD, the new Christmas festival took over from both the Sol Invictus and the older celebration of Saturnalia, the feast of Saturn. When the new religion took hold in Britain and Ireland, Christmas probably coincided with an older midwinter festival marking the beginning of the new year. By the middle ages, Christmas had become an extensive twelve-day festival, including both the feast of the nativity and the celebration of New Year.[8]

Early Christians did not know the date of Jesus' birth and could conveniently impose it upon existing pagan festivals. The date of his death was quite another matter, for it took place at a very definite time – during Passover, the ancient Jewish festival which celebrated the release of the Israelites from bondage in Egypt. During the fourth century AD, church authorities moved the date of the Easter festival so that it no longer

Ancestors of the Reiri family outside a whare puni at Mangaakuta, near Masterton, in the 1870s. In this decade, colonists began to outnumber Maori in the New Zealand population. Like all the images of Maori in this book, this photograph was taken by a European – in this case, Wellington photographer James Bragge. It reflects the vision of the colonisers as much as the culture of Maori.

F-4136-1/2, JAMES BRAGGE COLLECTION, ALEXANDER TURNBULL LIBRARY, WELLINGTON.

coincided with Passover, much as they had earlier made Sunday, rather than Saturday, their holy day. The Jews used a lunar calendar, the Romans a solar one. The date of Easter was now calculated using a combination of the two calendars, depending on both the equinox and the phase of the moon (the new measurement left some leeway for local interpretation, and Christians in different regions still use different dates for Easter). Easter, coming around the time of the northern hemisphere's spring equinox, may have coincided with earlier spring festivals, although scholars debate whether or not such a festival occurred in ancient Britain. The term Easter possibly derives from the name of an Anglo-Saxon goddess of the dawn. The festival of Jesus' resurrection occurring during spring may have been coincidental, but it was also highly appropriate, with nature at a peak of renewal just as Christians celebrated new life.[9]

The origins of our holidays are intriguing, but more interesting to historians is the way that holiday practices have changed over time and in different places. The mixture of people living in nineteenth-century New Zealand had a major impact on the evolution of holidays. Maori probably numbered around 100,000 at the time of Cook's 1769 exploration of New Zealand. By 1840 the introduction of muskets and new diseases had seen their population decline to 80,000 people and in the 1890s it reached its lowest ebb, around 42,000. Regional and iwi differences were great. Many more Maori lived in the north than the south, with about two-thirds of the population north of Taupo. In the mid-nineteenth century, the already small southern Maori population was still recovering from the devastating raids of Te Rauparaha, and Ngai Tahu were quickly overwhelmed, numerically at least, by the new European migrants. In the North Island, Maori outnumbered colonists until the 1870s, when the wars drew to an

OPPOSITE: Johann and Anna Heine celebrate their 50th wedding anniversary with family and friends from the German community in 1899. They arrived in New Zealand in 1850 to join the community near Nelson, Heine serving as Lutheran pastor. Their daughter Anna married another Lutheran pastor, Hartwig Dierks. G-32577-1/2, C. M. HEINE COLLECTION, ALEXANDER TURNBULL LIBRARY, WELLINGTON.

ABOVE: A Scandinavian gathering at the home of Honorary Danish Consul Sir Francis Bell, Lowry Bay, Wellington, in 1897. Many of New Zealand's Scandinavian migrants settled in Hawke's Bay. F-76847-1/2, HARKNESS COLLECTION, ALEXANDER TURNBULL LIBRARY, WELLINGTON.

end and immigration boomed. By the turn of the century, only the Bay of Plenty had more Maori than Pakeha residents.[10]

Between 40 and 50 per cent of nineteenth-century migrants were English-born – slightly more in the earlier years of settlement. Approximately 20 per cent came from Scotland and 18–19 per cent from Ireland. Of the rest, the largest numbers had been born in the Australian colonies, China and Germany; very few Welsh settled here. The new arrivals spread far and wide through the colony, but, as with the Maori population, there were some significant regional differences. Most notable was the southern dominance of the Scots. Although they could be found throughout the country, Scots settled especially in the south, attracted by the Scottish Free Church colony at Otago. Scots made up around 40 per cent of migrants to Otago and Southland, double the number of English, and in some rural districts they were a far higher proportion of the population. Canterbury and Taranaki were a little more English than other areas, and the West Coast more Irish. Some migrants from the smaller groups tended to cluster together – Chinese on the Otago and West Coast goldfields, Germans in Nelson and Scandinavians in Hawke's Bay.[11]

But country of origin can take us only so far in understanding the cultural baggage of migrants. Nineteenth-century Britain was as much a collection of disparate local cultures as a unified cultural whole. Residents in the north of England did things differently to those in the south, and Gaelic-speaking Highlanders lived very different lives from their compatriots on the Scottish Borders. New Zealand historians have recognised that we need to explore the regional specifics of New Zealand's 'British' heritage in order to understand the beginnings of Pakeha culture, and we are learning more about the origins of our forebears. Through the work of Terry Hearn we now know that migrants from Ireland to New Zealand came disproportionately from the far south (especially Counties Kerry and Cork) and the far north (especially County Antrim). County Dublin was also 'home' for a good number of Irish-born New Zealanders. Once 'invisible' migrants – such as Irish Protestants – are revealing themselves through statistical studies. Catholics were indeed the majority of Irish migrants to New Zealand, but only just. Protestants made up over 40 per cent of those coming here, most of them Anglicans in the earlier years of settlement, with Presbyterians dominating by the turn of the century.[12]

A significant proportion of English migrants to New Zealand came from three key regions in the south. London and its surrounding county provided a steady flow

William Cowling poses with some of his large family outside their home, Hurdon, Westown, New Plymouth, around the 1870s. Like many New Zealand migrants, Cowling came from humble origins in the south of England. He was born in Cornwall, possibly illegitimately, and worked as a quarryman prior to his migration in 1841. In Taranaki he took up farming and married Mary Hawke, another migrant from the south of England. PHO2004.211, PUKE ARIKI, NEW PLYMOUTH.

of migrants. A large number of artisans and farm workers from the home counties of Sussex, Kent, Hampshire, Surrey and Essex came to New Zealand in the 1870s, prompted by poor rural working conditions and increasing industrialisation. Economic decline in the south-west (Cornwall, Devon, Somerset, Dorset and Wiltshire), particularly relating to copper and tin mining, also drew many migrants. There had always been migrants from the north of England, but they were few compared to other regions. That changed around the turn of the century and especially from the 1920s, when northern England became an important source of migrants to New Zealand.[13]

In contrast to the Irish and English, the geographical origins of nineteenth-century migrants from Scotland to New Zealand bore a close resemblance to the regional

Erl and Elsie Clarke display their Scottish identity in this early twentieth-century photograph. They were born in New Zealand to parents who had migrated from Scotland as young children. Their father was from the north-west Highlands, son of a shepherd, and their mother was the daughter of a miner and a factory worker from Loanhead, near Edinburgh. Scottish migrants to New Zealand came from a wide range of social and geographic backgrounds. FROM THE AUTHOR'S COLLECTION.

spread of population in Scotland at the time. There were some small differences: a higher percentage of migrants came from the West Lowlands than might be expected, and a lower number from the Borders and South-west Scotland; Shetland Islanders had a particularly strong affinity with New Zealand. But, just as less than 10 per cent of Scots lived in the Highlands, so less than 10 per cent of Scottish migrants to New Zealand came from there, and the largest group (nearly 30 per cent) came from the most populous Scottish county, Lanarkshire (Glasgow and surrounding districts). All sorts of Scots came to New Zealand, from country and town, from industry and agriculture: the Scots, as a people, were particularly prone to emigration.[14]

Alongside national and regional background was another element that had a major impact on the evolution of holidays in New Zealand: religion. For a generation or so New Zealand's most prominent historians, influenced by their own secular perspectives, have tended to disregard the role of religion in the development of New Zealand culture.[15] In recent times scholars have been more willing to consider religion as an important feature of colonial society. Indeed, anyone who spends much time with sources which reveal the lives of nineteenth-century New Zealanders – letters, diaries, reminiscences and newspapers – cannot help but notice that religion was of huge significance to many individuals and most communities.

Non-believers were rare beasts in nineteenth-century New Zealand. In census after census only a tiny proportion – well under 1 per cent of the European population – declared that they had 'no religion'. A handful described themselves as Jews, Buddhists or Confucians but a huge majority – over 90 per cent – identified as Christians. These self-declared believers may not have practised their religion with the enthusiasm the clergy would have liked, but their belief still had an impact on the way they lived. Around 30–40 per cent of late nineteenth-century Pakeha New Zealanders were 'usual' church attenders; many others attended less regularly or only on special occasions, such as the festivals explored in this book. But religion did not solely mean churchgoing. Most people, whether or not they attended church, regarded Sunday as a day of rest, gave some sort of recognition to church festivals, attributed God with the control of the natural world and power over life and death, marked the rites of passage with Christian ceremonies, believed in heaven and gave their children some sort of Christian education.[16]

Just like 'Britishness', 'Christian' belief came in many varieties. Close to 90 per cent of late nineteenth-century European New Zealanders aligned themselves with the four largest churches. About 40 per cent were Anglican, 23 per cent Presbyterian, 14 per cent Roman Catholic and 10 per cent Methodist (they were divided into Wesleyans, Primitive Methodists and Bible Christians). Smaller churches included the Baptists (about 2 per cent), Lutherans and Congregationalists (about 1 per cent each); another 1 per cent or so belonged to Chinese religions, described in the census as 'Buddhists, Confucians, etc'. Jews, Quakers, Unitarians and others were much smaller groups.[17] Maori added to the strength of the Anglican, Catholic and Methodist churches, although this is harder to measure as the census did not collect information on Maori religious allegiance during the nineteenth century. Numbers of Maori Christians varied

A group of Maori Anglican clergymen photographed at East Cape about 1900. The Anglican Church was New Zealand's largest among both Maori and Pakeha. F-22632-1/2, M. ORBELL COLLECTION, ALEXANDER TURNBULL LIBRARY, WELLINGTON.

greatly with the effects of waves of conversion, missionary comings and goings, war and indigenous religious movements. As for Pakeha, the Anglican (Mihinare) Church attracted the largest number of Maori adherents, a reflection of the work of the Church Missionary Society, the Anglican movement which was first and largest of the missions to Maori.[18]

An individual's religious identification was often strongly linked to ethnic or geographic background, and just as the ethnic mix varied in different regions of the colony so did the religious mix. These differences persisted even decades after the original colonists had arrived. In Otago and Southland, where Scots dominated, so did Presbyterianism, accounting for over 40 per cent of European residents in the late nineteenth century. The Anglicans, the largest group elsewhere in the country, were correspondingly only 25 per cent. In rural districts like Taieri and Clutha the difference was even more marked, with well over half the population Presbyterian. Elsewhere, too, particular districts attracted higher than average allegiance for some religious groups. Methodism was strongest in Taranaki, Manawatu and North Canterbury – regions where large numbers of English labourers had settled – and Catholicism in Central Otago and on the West Coast.[19] Maori religious allegiance also varied widely by iwi and region.

Nineteenth-century New Zealand was clearly a place of considerable cultural complexity, and that demonstrated itself in different types of holiday keeping. Thomas Adam and his family, farming near Waihola in South Otago during the 1870s and 1880s, varied their work through the year according to the demands of the land and the seasons. Most years, 25 December found them carrying out a seasonal but hardly festive chore, carting manure from their dung heap to spread on the fields. Occasionally they took New Year's Day as a holiday, sailing on the nearby lake; Easter does not appear as a holiday in Thomas Adam's diary. But twice a year, without fail, in autumn and spring, Adam took a holiday for the most festive event in his world: the Presbyterian communion season.[20] Thomas Adam was no eccentric. A substantial minority of nineteenth-century colonists did not keep Christmas or Easter as holidays. Such behaviour appears odd to us now, when these festivals dominate our holiday calendar and seem to carry the weight of many generations of tradition. Why did these people, many of them devout Christians, not recognise the festivals surrounding the birth and death of Jesus, founder of their religion?

William Smaill had one simple but telling explanation. Recalling his childhood during the 1850s and 1860s on a South Otago farm, he noted: 'We did not keep Xmas Day as that was considered English at the time and we were Scotch'.[21] This ethnic difference was inseparably linked with religion. Scots were certainly no less devout than the English – in nineteenth-century New Zealand, Presbyterians were more diligent churchgoers than Anglicans.[22] Their differences over holidays stemmed from the Reformation of the sixteenth century, when the Protestant churches broke away from the Catholic. One of the many actions of the religious reformers was to modify the church calendar, which burgeoned with saints' days and festivals. The Lutheran churches on the Continent and the Anglican Church in England retained the holidays which marked events in the life of Jesus – his birth, death, resurrection and ascension to heaven. These festivals made up an annual cycle known as the 'Christian year'.

In the seventeenth century, some Protestants took this reform even further, purging the calendar of all festivals. The sermons and diaries of John Christie, a particularly conservative Presbyterian minister in the Otago rural parish of Waikouaiti, reveal the reasons behind these reforms, which he found convincing some two centuries later. Christie objected to the religious observance of Christmas for several reasons. He pointed out what scholars have long known: the date of Jesus' birth was uncertain, with 25 December an unlikely contender. The early church had left no record of a Christmas festival, and, crucially, there were 'no instructions in the Bible to keep such a day'. Christmas was thus 'a human invention' without 'scriptural authority'. That Anglicans and Catholics kept the festival was a further argument against it, in Christie's rather nationalist and sectarian opinion. He noted that Christmas and Easter received little attention in Scotland, for good historical reasons. Following attempts to 'force them into Popery and Prelacy', the Scots had endeavoured 'to discountenance what has been connected with these forms of religion', including the celebration of Easter and Christmas. Even worse, Christmas was grafted on to the old pagan festival of Yule, and there was no religious merit in observing a festival of 'heathen' origin.[23]

For English Puritans and Scottish Presbyterians, the religious calendar came to revolve not around the year, but around the seven-day cycle of the week. Keeping the Sabbath as a day of rest and worship became their great focus. English Puritans exported their rejection of the Christian year to the American colonies, and in Britain the Congregational and Baptist churches continued this tradition (members of these churches in New Zealand were as wary about the celebration of Easter and Christmas as the Presbyterians). In Scotland, Presbyterian dominance meant that Christmas and Easter were dropped from the calendar by the great majority of the population, although some festive (not religious) celebration did continue in earlier years, particularly in the Highlands. Christmas Day and Good Friday remained regular working days for many Scots as late as the 1950s.[24]

Before condemning nineteenth-century Scots and Presbyterians as boring killjoys, we should note that they kept one particularly lively holiday that the English and Irish did not: New Year. When they abandoned the Christmas religious festival, the Scots simply moved much of its associated revelry to New Year's Eve (known as 'Hogmanay') and New Year's Day. In 1876 a friend in Lincolnshire enquired of migrant Michael Cook, a sawmill worker and small farmer near Geraldine, if he 'kept Christmas up'. Cook replied, 'Of course we do, and we had green peas, new potatoes, and roast beef for dinner, and that will puzzle you at Pyewipe'. But what would have puzzled his former English labourer workmates more was his report that 'on New Year's day, no one here will work'.[25] For most nineteenth-century English residents, particularly those in the south, New Year was a regular working day, just as Christmas was for nineteenth-century Scots. The once extensive midwinter holidays of medieval England had been gradually pruned so that only Christmas Day, and sometimes Boxing Day, remained as days free from labour. Certainly many English people noted the passing of the old year and saw in the new, but often in a rather serious and sober way. In 1912 Clement Miles noted that 'New Year in England can hardly be called a popular festival; there is no public holiday and the occasion is more associated with penitential Watch Night services and good resolutions than with rejoicing'.[26]

It was not until the mid-twentieth century – around the same time that Scotland officially re-adopted the Christmas holiday – that New Year re-emerged as an English holiday. When it did so, it came as a Scottish import, bringing an entirely different flavour to the midwinter celebrations. Ronald Hutton provides a vivid description in his history of the British ritual calendar: 'Into the frequently cloying atmosphere of the Victorian Christmas, Hogmanay blew like a raw northern wind, smelling of alcohol. Its "natural" community was that of friendship, not family, and its deity was not Father Christmas but the more menacing one of Father Time.'[27] In Ireland, also, New Year was a less important holiday, kept most enthusiastically by migrants from Scotland until it became a more widespread festive occasion in the twentieth century.[28]

The relative freedom of colonial life allowed migrants, if they wished, to maintain their varied holiday traditions. Local businesses had considerable control over holidays, and if enough of them closed on a particular day it became a 'general holiday'. Provincial superintendents could create holidays by closing provincial government offices, and the governor could also declare holidays, either nationally or regionally. In practice, holidays were kept according to the common consent of the community, allowing for considerable individual and regional variation. On 29 January, Aucklanders commemorated the arrival of the colony's first governor, William Hobson, with an annual holiday. While the rest of the country worked, in the Queen City 'the gleesome bustle of folks, devoting themselves to holiday, might be heard in every street'.[29] In 1850 they held a 'Regatta of full and fair proportions', beginning a tradition which remains the anniversary's most notable feature.[30] But an attempt to make this a national holiday in 1890, the jubilee of British colonisation, proved a failure: each district had its own 'founding' event to commemorate.[31]

Holidays became more uniform towards the end of the nineteenth century, partly because New Zealanders began to adapt after several decades of living in ethnically and religiously diverse communities. Legislation also played a part, reflecting the growing bureaucracy of the period. New Zealand's first holiday legislation was the Bank Holidays Act (1873), closely modelled on the 1871 British Act and designed to allow bank workers to keep the same customary holidays as the rest of the public. Prior to this, bankers had been required to process transactions on every day except Sunday, Christmas Day and Good Friday, which were common-law holidays in England and Wales, although not in Scotland. In Britain, bank holidays became *de facto* public holidays, and the name still has this broader use there. The British Act had different schedules of holidays for England, Scotland and Ireland, recognising the different customs of each region. The New Zealand Act listed New Year's Day, Easter Monday, 24 May (Queen Victoria's birthday) and Boxing Day as holidays, with banks already closed on Christmas Day and Good Friday. In 1880 the Banks and Bankers Act, which covered many different areas of banking practice, extended the holiday schedule quite dramatically, although the public did not join bankers in having all these days off. The additional holidays comprised Easter Saturday, Whit-Monday (a popular English holiday associated with Whitsun, the religious festival of Pentecost, which fell seven weeks after Easter), 9 November (the Prince of Wales's birthday), and Saint Patrick's, Saint George's and Saint Andrew's Days.

Labour legislation, which tended to guarantee workers in a weak bargaining position the rights already obtained by others, sometimes also covered holidays. The Employment of Females Act (1873) entitled female factory workers to particular holidays (Christmas Day, New Year's Day, Good Friday, Easter Monday, 'and any other day set apart as a public holiday'), and the Factories Act (1894) extended the privilege to males under eighteen. Following the Industrial Conciliation and Arbitration Act (1894), a large variety of workers' awards included guaranteed holidays. The Labour Day Act (1899) created New Zealand's first statutory general holiday, legitimising an already popular practice.[32]

Not everyone was covered by holiday legislation, so customary practice remained important. Employers of domestic servants, for example, made their own rules, as did the self-employed. By the end of the century, in urban areas at least, the most widespread regular holidays were Christmas and Boxing Days, New Year's Day (and sometimes the day after), Good Friday and Easter Monday, the Queen's Birthday, Labour Day and the Prince of Wales's Birthday. Saint Patrick's Day was popular in some places, and until about the 1880s the residents of most districts in Otago had a holiday twice a year for the 'fast day' in preparation for Presbyterian communion. Each district had its own Anniversary Day or Show Day, and employers were also much more inclined than they are today to grant one-off holidays for special occasions, ranging from the Queen's Diamond Jubilee to the opening of a local bridge or railway. Paid annual leave was a twentieth-century development – for most nineteenth-century employees, time off was confined to public holidays. For the many people who worked six days a week, with only Sunday free, public holidays therefore had huge importance. Sunday recreation was controversial, so holidays were the only times when most workers had an entire day free for outdoor recreation or self-directed leisure. They seized the opportunity with enthusiasm.

In rural communities, though, Christmas and New Year proved inconvenient times for holidays. In the northern hemisphere they fell at the time when farm work was quietest: midwinter. It was a different matter altogether in New Zealand. In an era when even livestock farmers grew considerable amounts of grain to feed the horses which powered agriculture, harvesting was a huge task that sometimes fell around Christmas time. As a Poverty Bay resident recorded: 'Christmas has not been quite as gay and festive here as usual; people are too much in earnest building, harvesting &c, to spare much time for gaiety'.[33] Small farmers could manage their own working week and working year, taking holidays to suit themselves. It was not so easy when they had to employ others to help them, including seasonal workers like harvesters and shearers. For John Wither, farming sheep at Sunnyside near Queenstown, early January was shearing time. In 1880 he complained to his mother in Scotland about the trouble he had with the shearers: 'I found falt [sic] with 2 on new years day and although they could have made over one pound a day they left and it was two days before I could fill their places as the Races came off on the two days after the new year'.[34] In January 1879, a newspaper correspondent from Tuakau in South Auckland grumbled over what 'a very unfortunate time of the year it is to spend even one day in holiday-making, when the harvest is ripe for the sickle, and labour very scarce'. The local races, which attracted a large crowd on Boxing Day, might, he suggested, 'just as well have been held six weeks later, when the most busy and important season to the farmer will be over'.[35]

Other self-employed people took holidays when it suited them best, but custom clearly shaped their choices. On the goldfields, it quickly became the custom for miners to take a break at Christmas and New Year. As the *Otago Witness* explained in 1865: 'A few days holiday at Christmas has become an institution among miners, it being

THE BOSS SHEARER

'In the shearing shed', 1883. New Zealand farmers sometimes struggled to complete seasonal tasks, like shearing, because farm workers wanted holidays, like other workers, at Christmas and New Year. Engravings like this were used as newspaper illustrations until the turn of the century, when photographs took over. Some engravings bore a close resemblance to reality; others came straight from the artist's imagination. *ILLUSTRATED NEW ZEALAND NEWS*, 24 DECEMBER 1883, P. 4.

far more convenient for them to take a week or more right off once a year than a day now and then at shorter intervals – the great success of many operations being that the work should be continuous'.[36] On the Coromandel goldfields, the warden granted special protection for up to two weeks over Christmas and New Year, meaning miners could safely desert their claims for a holiday without fear of being 'jumped' by others. At Christmas 1867, two or three thousand made the trip from Thames to Auckland to be reunited with their families or just to enjoy the merrymaking on offer in the big town. Many also made the trip to Auckland at Easter, when special orders from the warden kept their claims protected from Good Friday through to Easter Monday, and in some years on the Tuesday after Easter as well.[37] Not everyone took a break. Some miners continued to work as usual at Christmas, particularly new arrivals and those yet to make a decent strike. In 1862 John Walker and his brother 'worked harder on Christmas day than usual'. Recently arrived at the Dunstan, they spent the day seeking a new place to try their luck and then began digging. As he wrote to his mother in England: 'We commenced a hole and tried the stuff soon after taking off the turf, found colour all the way down and both expected it to be either very or no good. It finally turned out to be the latter. Lost our camp and had to wander about 6 miles before we could find it'.[38]

School children were another group who often had extended holidays at Christmas, New Year and Easter. In the earlier years of European settlement, schools determined their own holidays, but later the regional boards of education exerted stricter control, not always with the approval of local school committees. In 1885, when the Auckland Education Board declared that schools should close from 18 December until 1 February, some schools thought this too long a time to take at once and rebelled against the order.[39] Many rural schools in the south preferred to take a shorter break at Christmas and a longer one at the time of the local grain harvest in February or March; if they did not have holidays then, they could expect low attendance. In March 1880 the *Palmerston & Waikouaiti Times* reported that most country schools in the district had closed for the harvest, 'some for a month and some for six weeks, in order that the farmers might have the assistance of their children at home'.[40] Others shortened their winter school holidays to cater for local needs. In 1887, Makotuku School Committee asked the Hawke's Bay Education Board for permission to take a week less holiday in winter so they could have a break in October. Children could then help out with the potato planting season without missing school.[41]

Those with several days free from work often took the opportunity to spend a few days away from home. Some went to a nearby town, but others preferred the delights of the wilderness. Frederick Barkas of Christchurch did not have the luxury of a break between Christmas and New Year from his work as a salesman with the New Zealand Loan and Mercantile Agency Company. He was determined, though, to make the most of the time he did have. In 1886 this extended from the evening of Christmas Eve until the morning of 28 December (27 December was kept as the Boxing Day holiday that year because 26 December fell on Sunday). Along with several other

The Westland family (Dolly, Peter, Mildred and Lady Janet) playing cards at their campsite, probably near Arthur's Pass, over Christmas and New Year of 1894–95. They were a prosperous family who could afford time off for leisure and enjoyed exploring the wilderness. CP 8410, 135-5&7, WESTLAND FAMILY ALBUM, A. C. GRAHAM COLLECTION, MACMILLAN BROWN LIBRARY, UNIVERSITY OF CANTERBURY.

young men – friends from his lodgings and his workplace – he spent Christmas under canvas on Banks Peninsula in an attempt to escape 'conventionalism and City Life'. Loaded with camping gear, fishing lines, guns and provisions they took a launch from Lyttelton to Port Levy, then hiked up to camp in native bush on the station belonging to 'Old Fleming'. Christmas dinner consisted of 'fried bacon & new potatoes cooked in the open air and eaten by the side of a chattering brook'. They enjoyed three idyllic days of rambling, sailing and fishing, and the evenings were more sociable than they had expected. They attended, somewhat reluctantly, a musical evening at the station homestead, and spent their last night at the Christmas ball given by local Ngai Tahu leader Hone Taare Tikao, whom they had met at the pa during their wanderings.[42]

Like Frederick Barkas, most working New Zealanders could expect at the most three consecutive days of holiday, and that only happened when their two-day Christmas or New Year holiday fell next to a Sunday. We now think of Easter as a continuous four-

Holidays were the best time for families to get together and celebrate. Here three generations of the Gorings, a Christchurch working-class family, gather for an unidentified special occasion about 1895. One of the young children is Mabel Howard, future trade unionist and labour politician (and New Zealand's first woman cabinet minister). S06-518B, E. J. HOWARD PAPERS, HOCKEN COLLECTIONS, UARE TAOKA O HAKENA, UNIVERSITY OF OTAGO.

day holiday, but in the nineteenth century most shop and factory workers considered it two separate holidays – Good Friday and Easter Monday – because they had to work on the Saturday between. The self-employed could take a longer break if they wished, and some generous employers gave their workers the Saturday off as well. In 1891 Dunedin bootmaker Jack Fowler tried to convince his boss to give the workers Easter Saturday off, and they would work Otago Anniversary Day (23 March, which fell close to Easter that year) instead. His employer refused this request and, as Fowler explained in a letter to his mother, 'I got a rough half hour for my trouble but I said that personally I did not care as one day was as good as another to me but there were some whose friends lived away who could then visit them if they had the three consecutive days'.[43]

Jack Fowler himself spent his holidays like many working New Zealanders of the nineteenth century. Sometimes he went on day excursions and picnics; on other occasions he attended local sporting events. His holiday experiences changed over time as he built up new links in the community to which he had migrated in his early twenties. Once he had met his future wife, Jeannie Broome, a machinist at the boot factory where he worked, she joined some of his holiday outings. Holidays later became a family affair, with Jack and Jeannie joining her parents and seven sisters for large festive meals, eventually bringing their own children to the extended family gatherings. Life stage clearly had an influence on individual holiday practice, alongside religion and ethnic background. Jack, a Londoner, had the fondness of an English migrant for the trappings of Christmas, though his Baptist faith meant he did not treat it as a religious holiday. Jeannie, born in New Zealand, had learned her religion and culture from her Scottish parents. As Presbyterians, they treated the holidays of the Christian year as occasions for recreation and family gatherings; Jack and Jeannie followed the same pattern.[44]

Different people kept holidays differently, and individuals changed their practice over time, but one thing about holidays did not alter: for almost all nineteenth-century New Zealanders they were the highlights of an existence generally dominated by hard work. In examining the holidays, we can come to understand more completely the lives of ordinary New Zealanders like Charles Hayward, Jack Fowler and Jeannie Broome. Examining the history of holidays offers us a richer portrayal of colonial life and also, more significantly, sheds light on some critical questions concerning our past. What sort of cultural and religious traditions did the great migration of the nineteenth century bring to Aotearoa? How did those traditions, which were many and varied, contrast and compete with one another, flourish or decline, merge or evolve in the multifaceted new cultural world of the colony? How did old-world traditions adapt to the different physical environment of the new? And what of the indigenous people – how did these imported traditions fit into their evolving culture? The three chapters which follow – detailed studies of Christmas, New Year and Easter – provide a window into the complex process of the making and shaping of New Zealand culture.

·⤳

CHAPTER ONE

Christmas

Christmas was one of the highlights of the Christian year for nineteenth-century Catholics, Anglicans and Methodists. In this, the 'feast of the nativity', they recalled the birth of Jesus, founder of their religion, with decorations and carols attracting many to the special festive services. But Christmas was always more than a church festival: it was a popular festival outside as well as within the churches. In many parts of Europe it was the great midwinter celebration – a time for feasting and revelry. Colonists brought all these elements of the northern-hemisphere festival with them to New Zealand, where Christmas had to adapt to a new season and a new social and cultural environment. But despite the necessity for adjustment in this new setting, Christmas remained closely identified with 'Englishness'. Although others joined them in keeping the holiday, it was New Zealand's largest group of migrants, the English, who found Christmas especially evocative of 'home'. Traditions of special significance for the English – roast beef, plum pudding and carolling, for instance – became entrenched as part of the New Zealand Christmas.

For other New Zealanders this was a less familiar holiday, but Maori and Scots eventually took up the Christmas celebrations of their neighbours (although many Scots remained wary about the religious elements of the holiday). This would evolve into a typically colonial holiday – a mixture of old-world winter customs and the summer foods and recreations of the southern hemisphere, and a complex amalgam of religious and secular traditions. But if Christmas came to be celebrated in a distinctly colonial way, it was by no means an isolated or nationalist celebration. By the end of the nineteenth century, in line with international trends, New Zealanders were beginning to adopt new Christmas customs such as the Christmas tree and Santa Claus from continental Europe and the United States. Christmas opens a window into the complex cultural world of nineteenth-century New Zealand.

When the holiday first reached these shores, though, it was a simple affair. Contrary to what generations of school children would later learn, the first Christmases celebrated in the islands that later became New Zealand were not religious ceremonies, but revelries. On Christmas Day 1642 the two ships of Dutch explorer Abel Janszoon Tasman were at anchor in what was to be called Cook Strait, waiting out bad weather and recovering from the shock of a fatal encounter with Ngati Tumatakokiri. They celebrated the festival with freshly killed pork from their on-board menagerie and extra rations of wine.[1] The English expedition led by James Cook celebrated Christmas 1769 aboard the *Endeavour*, sailing in heavy seas around the top of the North Island. They enjoyed 'Goose pye' made with gannets shot by Joseph Banks the previous day and spent Boxing Day nursing hangovers.[2] At the same time, further round the coast, Jean de Surville's French expedition lay anchored at Doubtless Bay. They left no record of Christmas festivities, but with the Dominican priest Paul-Antoine de Villefeix among their number, it is likely that they marked this important Catholic festival with a mass, which would have been New Zealand's first Christian service.[3] By the 1790s, exchange between the Maori and European worlds was growing. Entrepreneurs visited the country in search of merchandise and Maori adventurers sailed with them to visit the new penal colony at New South Wales, islands of the Pacific and even England. Sealers and whalers spent extended periods on shore, a few settling permanently. Christmas 1795 was celebrated at Dusky Sound by a motley crowd from two British vessels stopping off to collect seal fur and timber while on a voyage from Port Jackson (Sydney) to Bengal. The crew had a feast of pork and mutton, the passengers (who included former convicts and stowaways) had to settle for seal meat and fish; all enjoyed their share of spirits.[4]

These early Christmases reflected the importance of the festival in European culture, but they had little lasting impact. Christmas would not become a 'New Zealand' celebration – as opposed to a season observed by a few European visitors – until the early nineteenth century. Missionaries, traders, whalers, sailors and early colonists then introduced Maori to the two elements which made up the Christmas of their day: religious festival and riotous celebration.

On Christmas Day 1814 the Bay of Islands witnessed an historic religious service. Reverend Samuel Marsden, chaplain to the New South Wales penal colony, arrived at

Rangihoua shortly before Christmas to establish the country's first Christian mission. With him came the laymen who were to staff the mission – Thomas Kendall, John King and William Hall – along with their families and servants. On Christmas Day, a Sunday, Marsden conducted an Anglican church service on shore for a congregation which included several hundred Nga Puhi. Ruatara, a Nga Puhi leader who had spent considerable time with Marsden in Port Jackson, acted as translator, and the locals followed the lead of the visitors as they sat or stood at the appropriate times in the service. This was not the first time that Maori had attended a Christian service (several locals had been present when Hall read the service aboard the *Active* on a visit to assess the possibilities of the area for a mission station some months earlier; Ruatara and other Maori probably heard the service during their travels) but it heralded the beginning of the Christian mission to Aotearoa. Although it would be many years before more than a handful of Maori adopted the new religion, it marked the introduction of a phenomenon that would eventually have huge social, economic, cultural and spiritual significance for Maori. On that 1814 Christmas Day, Marsden preached from the words of the angels who brought to the Bethlehem shepherds the news of Jesus' birth: 'Behold I bring you good tidings of great joy'. It was a message appropriate for the Christmas season and also for the first preaching of the gospel in a new land.[5]

Over the next three decades Methodists and Catholics followed the Anglicans in establishing missions to Maori. Meanwhile, increasing numbers of European traders, whalers, entrepreneurs and drifters arrived in the country, forerunners of the settlers who migrated in their thousands after New Zealand became a British colony in 1840. Migrants and visitors from England, Ireland and continental Europe celebrated Christmas, where possible, in the way most familiar to them – with lavish eating and drinking. In 1848 the newly established village of Dunedin experienced a rowdy Christmas. Tom Watson of the Commercial Hotel invited 'all and sundry' to a free Christmas dinner and a 'great gathering' of locals, supplemented by 30 visiting American whalers, took up his invitation. Drink flowed freely after the meal and all enjoyed themselves until a runaway sailor mischievously selected as his musical contribution to the party 'The Battle of the *Shannon* and *Chesapeake*' (a ballad celebrating the victory of a Royal Navy frigate over a United States frigate at Boston in 1813). This proved 'a most unlucky selection for such a mixed company' and fighting soon broke out, quickly degenerating into a free for all.[6] Sailors seem to have been particularly prone to Christmas drinking sprees, making the most of any break from their harsh working life. In 1831 missionary Henry Williams, visiting Kororareka on Christmas Day, reported 'Numbers of sailors rolling about the beach in a most disgraceful state using most horrible language'.[7]

Drunken sailors were simply an exaggerated example of the most common way of celebrating Christmas in early nineteenth-century England. During Queen Victoria's reign (1837–1901) the English Christmas developed into the festival centred on children and the family that many now consider 'traditional'. But in earlier decades Christmas had been a much rowdier community event which featured, alongside special church services, various forms of carnival and misrule, with the swapping of roles between children and adults, men and women, and masters and servants. Above all, it was a time for eating and drinking in abundance, when landowners provided feasts for their tenants, the rich gave to the poor and workers expected treats from their employers.[8]

The missionaries also enjoyed communal Christmas feasts. James West Stack, brought up on various North Island Anglican mission stations in the 1830s and 1840s, recalled that at Te Papa, near Tauranga, it was the custom for 'the whole mission staff to dine together on Christmas Day at Mr Brown's, and all the children old enough to sit on ordinary chairs were allowed to join their elders'. New Zealand-born Stack was teased for not being an Englishman when he chose cold raspberry tart over hot plum pudding the first time he was old enough to join the feast.[9] In the early 1840s at the southern Wesleyan mission station at Waikouaiti, Otago, missionary James Watkin marked the Christmas festival with extra church services, sometimes incorporating the baptism of Kai Tahu converts or a Methodist 'lovefeast' (a communal meal where all drank water from a common 'loving-cup' and shared spiritual testimonies). In 1842 he added to the celebrations by giving a feast for Kai Tahu on 26 December.[10]

The English tradition of communal feasting at Christmas fitted well into Maori traditions of hospitality. The hakari (feast) remains an important feature of modern hui, generally as the closing event of the gathering. In the nineteenth century, though, the hakari could be the sole reason for a hui, with chiefs arranging magnificent feasts to demonstrate their wealth and mana.[11] Maori associated with the various mission stations joined their Christmas festivities, as at the Wesleyan Mission at Waima, Hokianga, in 1863. A large crowd gathered there for a Christmas church service followed by a large feast of English-style food, cooked by Nga Puhi women under the direction of the missionary's wife. They ate outdoors at large tables under an oak tree decorated with flags and streamers and followed the meal with speeches and games.[12] Away from

A meal at an unidentified hui around the 1890s. PACOLL-5932-08, ALEXANDER TURNBULL LIBRARY, WELLINGTON.

'Christmas Preparations', illustration by an unknown artist from *New Zealand Graphic*, 29 December 1894. PUBL-0109-1894-611, ALEXANDER TURNBULL LIBRARY, WELLINGTON.

the mission stations, Christian Maori arranged their own Christmas hakari, with Pakeha frequently joining the occasions as guests. In 1859 Henare Haratana and other Maori at Mahurangi (south of Warkworth) gave a feast 'on the great day of the birth of our Lord' for 70 people, among them several Pakeha.[13] Such Christmas feasts invariably included speech making, with outdoor sports and sometimes dancing to follow.

At Parikino, on the Whanganui River, Christmas dinner was one of several highlights at a large 1875 hui attended by 800 to 1000 people, 'the largest assembly of Maoris ever held in that place'. The great hui included, in addition to the Christmas festivities, distribution of prizes to school children, the baptism of over 50 children and the weddings of about 40 couples.[14] The Christmas feast given in 1880 by Ngati Te Ata leader Henare Kaihau at Tahurangatira, on the Manukau Harbour, was a more

MAORIS PREPARING CHRISTMAS DINNER.

Maori preparing a feast for Christmas dinner around the turn of the century. Postcard printed by Spreckley & Co. Booksellers, Auckland, and sent from Kenneth of Clevedon to Charlie Robertson in London, 1903. FROM THE AUTHOR'S COLLECTION.

traditional display of chiefly mana. About 300 people attended this magnificent hakari, where '10 sheep, quarter of a bullock, a like number of pigs, fish, oysters, vegetables, and innumerable cakes and puddings, not forgetting a liberal supply of beer, wine, and spirits, were provided, and liberally dispensed to all comers'. The guests included Maori and Pakeha, Christians and Hauhau (followers of Pai Marire, a Maori religious movement).[15] These large Christmas feasts involved extensive preparations by the entire host community, as the *New Zealand Graphic*'s 1894 illustration of 'Christmas Preparations' suggests. Children gathered eels, a local delicacy which sat alongside the English Christmas favourites of roast beef and plum pudding at the festive meal.

By the late nineteenth century Maori, sailors and missionaries were all minority groups in a New Zealand dominated by colonists and their descendants. Although Scottish migrants had little experience of Christmas, English colonists kept their most important holiday with vigour. Christmas was also a key event, being above all a religious holiday, for the Irish (with the notable exception of Irish Presbyterians, who, like their Scottish counterparts, did not keep Christmas as a religious occasion).[16] As a Catholic and Anglican church festival, Christmas came second only to Easter. Many Methodists, too, observed the church festival. Over 60 per cent of the Pakeha population belonged to these three denominations, and they also accounted for most Maori Christians. Not all, though, were regular churchgoers. Anglicans were the least diligent in attending church: less than a third counted as 'usual attendees' and many went only occasionally.[17]

Although many Christians did not go to church often, Christmas services attracted large congregations. Vicesimus Lush, vicar of All Saints' Anglican Church in the military settlement of Howick, commented at Christmas 1851 on the 'excellent congregation, the first really good *voluntary* one since I have been here' (usually, in his parish, a large congregation meant a compulsory church parade for the local Fencibles, the British military settlers).[18] In some more remote or newly settled districts, church services were few and far between. Mr Ball, the first preacher to visit the district of Huia, in the Waitakeres, for nine months, commented to his schoolhouse congregation on the Sunday following Christmas Day 1896 that 'in such a place as the Huia, where service is seldom held, people were very apt to forget the first Christmas, and think of the present Christmas simply as a time of amusement'.[19] Generally, however, the residents of country districts recognised the special religious significance of Christmas. At Omaha, another small settlement near Auckland, the celebrations for Christmas 1878 included carol singing in the decorated schoolroom on Christmas Eve, while on Christmas morning 'our district schoolmaster read the Church of England service in an impressive style'.[20]

Why did so many people crowd city cathedrals and pack country schoolhouses for Christmas services? What attracted, for example, the 800 people who attended midnight mass, with a further 150 unable to squeeze in, at St Patrick's Catholic Cathedral, Auckland, in 1868?[21] What about the 220 people who attended the 1881 Christmas services at St Peter's Anglican Church, in the Dunedin suburb of Caversham?[22] For the devout, this was a very special occasion, one of the spiritual highlights of the year. It was a time to hear again the familiar story of the baby Jesus, born in the humblest of circumstances yet worshipped as the son of God; a child whose birth was surrounded by marvellous signs, by angels and shepherds, stars and wise men from the east. It was a time for Christians to celebrate the miracle of the Incarnation: that God had come to live on earth amongst ordinary humans.

But not all attended Christmas services for their spiritual significance. A reporter commenting on the large congregations at the 1882 Anglican Christmas services in the Otago villages of Palmerston and Waikouaiti noted that some people were 'attracted to the services from mere curiosity, while others go there with a more commendable object, and are impelled there by religious fervour'.[23] Curiosity no doubt drew some of the 800 attending the St Patrick's midnight mass at Auckland in 1868, for they included 'persons of all denominations'.[24] On Christmas Eve 1871 Frank Barraud, a young Wellington Anglican, and a group of friends 'went to see the midnight mass at the Roman Catholic Cathedral there was an awful crush to get in at the door, we came away about half past one before the mass was finished'.[25]

Certainly there was much at such services to attract the curious. One of the chief attractions was the special Christmas music. Choirs and soloists made a special effort for the occasion, often with very good results. 'The services were as musical and joyous as we could make them and I think I have never heard the choir sing better', Vicesimus Lush reported of Christmas 1876 at St George's Anglican Church, Thames.[26] At St Joseph's, Dunedin, music at the Christmas high mass in 1873 featured selections from masses by Haydn, Gounod and Mozart, the 'Hallelujah Chorus' and 'Adeste Fideles'.[27] 'Adeste Fideles' – 'O Come All Ye Faithful' – was the most popular Christmas hymn. At the St Joseph's Christmas midnight mass in 1894, we can imagine the effect upon the huge but profoundly still congregation, some crowding out into the porch of the beautifully decorated church, as the Angelus rung out at midnight and, following the opening prayer, the choir burst into song with the familiar call to come and behold the child born at Bethlehem.[28] This hymn was popular in Protestant as well as Catholic churches. At Trinity Wesleyan Church, Dunedin, the 1879 Christmas morning service included 'an additional attraction in the shape of a band of our best instrumentalists'. Among them was Charles Waud, who 'will play as a violincello solo the Christmas anthem "Adeste Fideles"'.[29]

Christmas hymns and carols achieved unprecedented popularity in the late nineteenth century. Enthusiasts revived old songs, wrote new songs and translated others from Latin or modern European languages. 'While Shepherds Watched their

The Anglican Church of the Holy Sepulchre, Khyber Pass, Auckland, decorated for Christmas 1891. A description in the *New Zealand Herald* reveals that the decorations featured the colours green, white and red. The lattice work was decorated with greenery and the cross at the top made of scarlet geraniums; on the altar were 'four handsome vases of red and white flowers'. Decorations in the rest of the church, not visible in this photograph, included ropes of evergreen encircling the pillars and ivy leaves outlining doors and windows. C22785, AUCKLAND WAR MEMORIAL MUSEUM

Flocks' (a paraphrase from the gospel) was the first Christmas hymn, indeed the first hymn, formally approved by the Church of England, being added to the official collection of metrical psalms in 1700. Eighteenth-century additions to the popular Christmas repertoire included, amongst others, 'Christians Awake, Salute the Happy Morn' and Charles Welsey's 'Hark the Herald Angels Sing'. The nineteenth century popularised many new compositions, including 'Once in Royal David's City', 'O Little Town of Bethlehem' and 'We Three Kings'. John Mason Neale, who wrote many hymns, including 'Good Christian Men Rejoice', also translated ancient songs, among them the Christmas hymn 'Of the Father's Love Begotten'. Others translated popular European carols such as 'Silent Night' into English.[30]

Congregations loved singing Christmas carols and their leaders encouraged the practice. In 1876, St Matthew's Anglican Church, Dunedin, began what quickly became a very popular annual practice: a Christmas Eve carol service, with a combined choir

In 1878 E. A. C. Thomas photographed this Anglican country church, probably at Motueka, decorated for Christmas. He later painted over the image to highlight the red flowers interspersed through the abundant green foliage. Country churches were as much a part of the decorating tradition as their urban counterparts. E-305-Q-003, ALEXANDER TURNBULL LIBRARY, WELLINGTON.

from various Anglican churches. Bishop Samuel Nevill spoke to the congregation on 'the importance and advantages of Carol singing at Christmastide', referring to 'its time-honoured observance in the old country'.[31] In 1880 Edward Benson, Anglican Bishop of Truro in Cornwall, devised a new form of Christmas service, the Festival of Nine Lessons and Carols, which interspersed Bible readings with carols.[32] This caught on quickly, no doubt partly assisted by Benson's promotion to Archbishop of Canterbury, the world leader of the Anglican church, in 1883. In that same year, the new form of service was sanctioned by the Bishop of Auckland and Christmas Eve 1883 saw a large crowd gathered for the special festival at St Mary's Church, Parnell. The service 'appeared to find special acceptance with the congregation'.[33]

Decorations further added to the appeal of Christmas services, with greenery, flowers and fabric or floral texts adorning most Anglican and Catholic churches. In 1870 Frank Barraud noted that Wellington's St Paul's Anglican Cathedral was 'decorated with nikau leaves & flowers & bands of leaves round the pillars'. He was less complimentary about 'a sort of arched screen across the chancel, with a large white cross on the top, which I do not think added to the beauty of the church'.[34] Seasonal church decoration reached elaborate heights in the late Victorian period and New Zealand's Catholic and Anglican churches participated fully in the fashion.[35] In 1878 Anglican churchgoers in Auckland could gaze at the 'very elegant appearance' of St Paul's Cathedral, where the 'organ loft, the baptistery, the entrance to the vestry, were hung with wreaths of fern branches and scarlet geraniums. A large star of elegant form was set over the communion table, and similar devices ornamented the pulpit.' Or maybe they would have preferred to visit St Matthew's Church, where the 'pillars of the church were festooned with garlands of flowers and evergreens in spiral wreaths, and the chancel, pulpit, organ and baptismal font were also decorated, the brilliant pohutukawa blossoms shewing out in bright profusion amongst the evergreens'.[36] At Dunedin's St Joseph's Catholic Cathedral in 1891 the 'arrangement of immense quantities of beautiful flowers, white lilies predominating, and their tasteful disposal among the numerous lights and ornamental candlesticks, especially in the evening, was dazzlingly effective'.[37] A similar abundance of tapers, white lilies and garlands can be seen in the illustration of the old St Mary's Catholic Cathedral, Wellington.

English historian Ronald Hutton has noted 'certain perpetual patterns' which the rhythms of the year impose on calendar customs, including a yearning for light and greenery in midwinter and for symbols of rebirth at spring.[38] For New Zealand colonists, any special craving for greenery at Christmas came not from the season but from the desire to import a much-loved practice from their source cultures, just one of many attempts to make themselves at home in their new environment. In the southern hemisphere, though, because of the opposite seasons they could not easily use the foliage traditionally associated with Christmas. Adding to their woes, in the early years of colonisation traditional European plants were seldom available in sufficient quantity for decorations. New Zealanders seized, therefore, on local plants to replace those which had adorned their churches in Europe. Charlotte Godley, wife of Canterbury founder John Godley, wrote to her mother in 1850, describing her first Christmas in Christchurch: 'We had a few greens for the Church, but not enough, and we had a few up, too, in the rooms, but although they are evergreens, they die like our ordinary trees, and will not last, like our good holly and ivy and laurel, till Twelfth Night'.[39]

St Mary's Catholic Cathedral, Wellington, decorated for Christmas. The date is unknown, but must have been before fire destroyed the building in November 1898. CATHOLIC ARCHDIOCESAN ARCHIVES, WELLINGTON

The holly, with its magnificent winter berries, was an iconic Christmas plant, providing the distinctive Christmas colours of green and red. In New Zealand, though, it was not in fruit in December, leading the colonists to seek out other suitable decorative plants. In the north of the country there was an obvious solution. The Howick vicar Vicesimus Lush and his sons simply visited the beach 'for Pohutukawas (our Xmas tree – our substitute for holly)'.[40] At St Paul's Cathedral, Auckland, in 1897, the Christmas decorations included 'lilies, roses, cosmos, and stocks (all white)', but the 'lectern was decked with cabbage palms, flax, and pohutukawa, a really New Zealand decoration'.[41] Such use of native flora was not simply a matter of developing national identity: it represented part of the process Peter Gibbons has described as 'cultural colonisation', the ongoing adoption of indigenous phenomena into Pakeha culture.[42]

Not everyone found these local substitutes satisfactory, retaining deep, nostalgic memories of Christmas in England. Eliza Jones, after sneaking a peek at the decorations at Auckland's St Paul's on Christmas Eve 1857, commented that the 'tree fern fronds looked beautiful in the niches of the church but the crimson flowered pohutukawa but ill supplied the place of our dear English holly, especially as it is not at all sweet scented, but rather the reverse'.[43] In the south of the country, where pohutukawa did not grow wild (and, if cultivated, did not flower until after Christmas), church decorators sought other substitutes for red holly berries. Catholic Archbishop Francis Redwood had fond memories of his first communion, taken at the 1851 Christmas midnight mass at Nelson. Under the guidance of Father Anthony Garin, he and the others preparing for the sacrament decorated 'the little lowly, unlined wooden chapel (no larger than a good sized room) with ripe cherries and roses, making such sentences as Gloria in excelsis Deo [glory to God in the highest], and such like'.[44]

Decorating churches for Christmas was a labour of love, often carried out by women of the congregation. At St Joseph's Cathedral, Dunedin, the Dominican nuns prepared the ornate decorations. Children, too, took part. Emma Allen recalled that she and her sister Carrie, living on a farm at Waiwhetu in the Hutt Valley during their 1860s childhood, helped decorate the Anglican church for Christmas. They would 'carry out a clothes basket full of lovely flowers from my mothers lovely garden for helping with the decorations . . . we used to help in making long wreaths of greenery to twine round the Pillars all sorts of Flowers were used for decorations in those days'.[45] This was clearly an enjoyable task, but it also involved hard work. On Christmas Eve 1883, anyone passing All Saints' Anglican Church, Ponsonby, could tell that something was afoot: 'Workers assembled as early as nine o'clock, and from that time until ten o'clock in the evening there was one continual buzz of voices in the schoolroom, and the sound of footsteps and soft whispers in the church . . . . At six o'clock on Christmas morning helpers were at work renewing and reviving the decorations.'[46] Considerable organisation was also needed. At Thames, in 1868, Mrs Mackay and Vicesimus Lush arranged for 'a few of the leading members of the Aquatic Club . . . to go out in their boat for Nikau palms and tree fern leaves – Karaka leaves and Rata flowers for the Church. The gentlemen seemed rather pleased than otherwise at the job.' Christmas morning found Lush 'early at the church, placing in various places the flowers Mrs Goodall sent me last night – flowers she had imported on purpose from Parnell'.[47]

Anglican churches tended to have the most ornate decorations of greenery and flowers, but many Catholic churches had an additional attraction at Christmas: the crib. The crib or nativity scene was first created by St Francis of Assisi in the thirteenth century to vividly display the simplicity, poverty and humility of Jesus' birth, with his bed a manger filled with hay and an ox and an ass standing by. At St Benedict's, Auckland, in 1886, 'a distinctive feature of the Christmas attractions' was 'a representation of the stable of Bethlehem', which had been 'erected in a very pretty style by one of the brothers'.[48] New Zealand churches do not seem to have used the live animals which featured in St Francis's original crib, but they did have figures available to create impressive nativity scenes. In 1885 Dunedin's Dominican sisters set up a crib in their convent, which adjoined the cathedral, using 'new and beautiful images of the Holy Family' imported from Europe. This attracted numerous visitors.[49] In later years the sisters' crib appeared in the cathedral itself where it fulfilled St Francis's wishes by providing 'a touching representation of the great event at Bethlehem', forming 'the object of devotion of large numbers of the congregation' through the week of Christmas. The scene was a cave with the baby lying on a bed of straw, Mary and Joseph kneeling in adoration on either side.[50]

Many nineteenth-century Anglicans regarded this behaviour with suspicion. The crib was a little too Catholic, a little too redolent of the worship of images, for them to accept with comfort. Attitudes slowly changed and during the twentieth century cribs became popular in Anglican churches also. By the late twentieth century even the most conservative Protestants happily displayed nativity scenes in their churches and homes. Back in the nineteenth century, though, Presbyterians, Baptists and Congregationalists remained wary about the concept of Christmas itself (Wesleyans and other Methodists generally held Christmas services, but without the decorations and fanfare of Anglicans and Catholics). In districts where Scots predominated, Christmas had little impact, many rural families continuing their usual workaday activities.

In more urban areas, Scots encountered the Christmas-keeping of migrants from other places. By 1860 Christmas had become a holiday in Dunedin, with government operations closed according to precedents in England, where Christmas was a common-law holiday. Businesses began closing for Christmas and the Anglican Church, which boasted a resident clergyman from 1852, observed this important holy day.[51] How were Scots to keep this unaccustomed holiday? If Presbyterian, they certainly did not treat it as a religious occasion. That would have been a concession to ritualist or Catholic practice. Instead, family gatherings and outdoor recreation became the order of the day. George Hepburn, a Dunedin merchant and Presbyterian elder, wrote to his family in Fifeshire of the strange new custom. In 1858 he noted that 'last Saturday being Christmas was held as an holy day. Shops all shut, – so we had a family party at

Waikari [*sic*] . . . in all 17 sat at dinner, all very happy not forgetting absent friends.' Nine years later he wrote to his sister, 'On Christmas day last, as is our usual we had all our friends at our house <u>thirty five</u> in number . . . the day being fine they all seemed to enjoy themselves, – Ch[ristma]s is held a complete holiday here, except the English church morning service'.[52] The Hepburn extended family always gathered again at New Year for a more familiar holiday. Other Scottish colonists took part in organised excursions on Christmas Day, such as the harbour cruises offered in Dunedin in 1856.[53]

Towards the end of the nineteenth century, some Protestants began to question why their churches avoided the religious celebration of Christmas. After all, as Donald Stuart, the popular minister of Dunedin's Knox Church pointed out in the *N. Z. Presbyterian* magazine in 1891,

> The Presbyterians of these colonies . . . are compelled to observe this day as a holiday. Now, is there not something incongruous, or worse than incongruous, in observing as a mere holiday the day on which all other Christians commemorate such a momentous event as the birth of Christ   the central fact in the history of the universe?[54]

As conservative Calvinism gave way to a more emotive evangelicalism in some Protestant congregations, Christmas gained a new appeal. In 1885 St Andrew's Presbyterian Church, Dunedin, held an early-morning Christmas service and in the same year even conservative minister William Will enjoyed a special 'service of praise' given by the choir on Christmas Eve in East Taieri Presbyterian Church.[55] From the 1870s, Baptists in Auckland could attend the special Christmas 'flower service' at their Wellesley Street Church, the congregation bringing bouquets of flowers to be passed on to public institutions such as the refuges for elderly men and women.[56] Auckland Congregationalists, rather than holding a Christmas service, began in the 1880s to mark the festival with a regular Christmas Day performance of Handel's *Messiah* in their Beresford Street Church.[57]

Others continued the resistance to Christmas frivolities. In 1891 the staunch Presbyterian elders of Dunedin's First Church refused their minister's request to hold a Christmas service, and their organist's request to play carols in the church on Christmas evening.[58] But the times were changing, and in the early decades of the twentieth century more and more Protestant congregations began to hold Christmas services, with the New Zealand Presbyterian Church finally giving its official approval to the practice in 1932.[59] By the mid-twentieth century, with more Protestant churches recognising the festival, a far greater proportion of New Zealanders observed Christmas as a religious occasion than had in the nineteenth century.

· ᴗ

But Christmas was always more than a religious festival, and those who celebrated Christmas at church also did so at home and in their communities. Religion was not, of course, confined to churches. Carols, for example, were as often heard in the streets as they were in formal places of worship. Carollers, still often known by the old English term of 'waits', wandered the streets of New Zealand towns on Christmas Eve, sometimes singing right through the night. In 1857 the residents of Wellington, 'who are not often awoke out of their first sleep with any degree of satisfaction', heard 'performances of the "Waits"', the choir of the Wesleyan Church singing carols.[60] Young Ellen and Alice Windsor of Napier 'would beg Mother to waken us to hear the carol singers and the band when they came near, late on Christmas Eve'.[61] Others were woken whether they liked it or not. In 1876, Thames vicar Vicesimus Lush went to bed after a busy day of preparations for the Christmas festival but, shortly after falling asleep, 'woke to a large party of men singing carols in the road opposite our bedroom windows. Again I went to sleep and a second time was disturbed by a party of men and women who sang carols, accompanied by some musical instrument and the effect I thought was good.' That good effect was 'nothing equal to a third party of *Cornishmen* who for the third time woke me up out of my sleep by singing carols! So nicely that it was quite a pleasure to listen to them.'[62]

Some carollers raised funds by soliciting donations as they went on their rounds. In 1876 a band of ten singers and 'a harmonium (carried about on trestles), piccolo, flute, bass viol, and two violins' from Franklin Road Primitive Methodist Chapel wandered the streets of Auckland from midnight until seven in the morning, 'in the first place to usher in fittingly Christmas morn, by carolling, and in the second to raise funds for the benefit of the new chapel in that district'.[63] In 1899 the Protestant Band raised £42 for their uniform fund by parading the streets of Timaru, while the local Salvation Army Band collected £20 the same way.[64] Others were offered refreshments by appreciative householders. Some church choirs who went carolling had an explicitly evangelistic purpose. In 1883 the *New Zealand Herald* grumbled that 'old carols seem to have lost their time-honoured celebrity, and have given place to Moody and Sankey', popular evangelical songs of the day.[65]

For many New Zealanders carolling was, above all, a celebration of Englishness. In 1877 a band of young men calling themselves the Orpheus Carol Party entertained the residents of Auckland by 'singing the fine old carols so dear to English people'.[66] When the inhabitants of Palmerston, Otago, woke to the sound of carollers in 1882, the 'surprise proved both pleasing and welcome, and no doubt recalled a most cherished scene and incidents of Home land'.[67] English migrants rarely formed the ethnic organisations so popular with the Scots, who had their Burns Clubs and Caledonian and St Andrew's Societies, and the Irish, with their Hibernian Societies. The English colonists, who formed the majority culture in New Zealand, apparently felt little need to assert their ethnic identity. Englishness was, to them, normal; ethnic display belonged to other cultures. This makes it all the more intriguing that those few English migrants who did form cultural groups (which were generally regional, reflecting one district of the motherland, rather than national) indulged in carolling. At Christmas 1877 in Dunedin, the 'members of the Yorkshire Club met at the Empire Hotel on the 24th and ushered in Christmas Day after the way of the people of their native country. They afterwards sallied forth and treated their fellow citizens to a number of carols and glees, which were very well sung.'[68] Likewise, it was a group of Cornishmen who serenaded Vicesimus Lush with carols on Christmas Eve 1876 in Thames, while the 'Cornish Singers' who treated the inhabitants of Auckland to Christmas carols in 1875 may also have come from Thames, many miners having travelled to the city for the holiday.[69]

Carols fitted readily into the new colonial environment, but other elements of the English Christmas felt quite out of place. As an anonymous *Otago Witness* columnist explained in 1881, 'it is not easy to keep up the good old customs of the lands we have left . . . . All the pleasant customs which cluster about Christmas-tide presuppose the biting cold, the low-hung skies, the short days, the spectral snow-draped landscape of a northern winter.'[70] The same writer declared some years later, 'Christmas comes at midsummer, which is much the same thing as not coming at all'. Indeed, 'without snow on the ground and icicles at the eaves, without "the Yule log sparkling on the hearth" and the mistletoe pendant in the hall, Christmas is not Christmas, but a hollow make-believe'.[71] Samuel Stephens, a New Zealand Company surveyor who settled in the Nelson district, noted in his diary for 1853 that Christmas Day was 'as in England a general holiday, but in no way realising that festive season, in consequence of the totally opposite character of the seasons'.[72]

Such comments, which recur frequently in New Zealand newspapers, diaries and letters throughout the nineteenth century, should not be dismissed as insignificant clichés. For migrants from northern Europe, Christmas was inextricably linked with winter, and the experience of a New Zealand summer Christmas highlighted the 'strangeness' of their new home. Jemima Martin wrote from her farm at Tamaki to her sister in England: 'The change of seasons, Xmas in the middle of summer & winter in August gives one an uncomfortable sensation of being turned upside down & I cannot get over it & don't think I ever shall'.[73] Thomas Ferens, a young teacher at the Wesleyan mission in Waikouaiti, Otago, explained the huge impact this change of seasons had on migrants in an 1850 letter to England:

> No one has any idea what strange changes come over an individual in a New Country. Oh how altered every subject is looked upon out here, there being a reverse of seasons, which materially changes your old ideas & habits on that point – then comes Christmas in Summer &c all these things you don't at the time think about, and the period passes away without any particular interest, because you have not been thinking and expecting to meet them as was wont. Old association of ideas do not exist out here.[74]

Some migrants found the heat of a southern Christmas distinctly uncomfortable. One of them was James 'Snyder' Brown, editor of the *New Zealand Herald*, whose holiday editorials in the early 1870s had a distinctly negative tone. 'The holidays have been carried through in true British fashion', he declared early in 1873. 'Much eating, copious drinking, violent exercise, followed by fatigues and prostration of the body, appears to be considered the right way of spending one's time at a season of the year when the sun is nearly vertical, and when prudence and an observance of hygeian precautions would suggest the necessity of rest amid quiet retreats.' He did not begrudge workers their holidays, but felt they were 'of the wrong sort, at the wrong

The cover of the *Weekly News* Christmas supplement, 1874, portrayed the joys of Christmas in summer. The picture appeared on the cover of the *Illustrated Sydney News* ten years earlier, hence the reference to Australia – this was an image that apparently held appeal for all southern-hemisphere colonists.

time of the year. We ignore the beautiful autumn and spring days, at which time out-of-door exercise would renew the jaded elasticity of the body and banish fatigue and worry of mind.'[75]

Others were pleased with the novelty of a summer Christmas and revelled in its opportunities. It might be difficult, declared the *Otago Witness* in 1858, to recognise old Christmas in this more genial clime, 'his hair bound with garlands of summer flowers, his robes of verdure loosely flowing in the summer's breeze, bearing in his hands and dropping in his path the choice fruits, the cherry and strawberry, the currant and gooseberry. But can you not welcome him all the more heartily?'[76] Likewise, in Hokitika, old Father Christmas arrived 'surrounded by all the glory and beauty of an Austral summer'.[77] In 1874 Auckland's *Weekly News* portrayed the change on the cover of its Christmas supplement. Old Father Christmas fades into the background,

'How we spent our Christmas' celebrated the joys of outdoor amusement during a New Zealand Christmas. *ILLUSTRATED NEW ZEALAND HERALD*, 11 FEBRUARY 1878, P. 12.

TOP: A Christmas card produced by the firm A. D. Willis of Wanganui around 1886, portraying the White Terraces recently destroyed by the eruption of Mt Tarawera. E-068-003, ALEXANDER TURNBULL LIBRARY, WELLINGTON.

BOTTOM: Saunders, McBeath & Co. of Dunedin produced this Christmas card, with its portrayal of scenic wonders (painted by Nathaniel Leves) and summer flowers, in 1882. The verse on the back commented on the differences between a northern- and southern-hemisphere Christmas. DC-0311, OTAGO SETTLERS MUSEUM, DUNEDIN.

superseded by a beautiful young woman with summer flowers in her hair and summer fruits around her. The figures below include, alongside those bearing traditional Christmas foods, people enjoying the outdoor sports possible on a southern Christmas Day. Outdoor sports also featured in the *Illustrated New Zealand Herald*'s 'How we spent our Christmas'.

Illustrated newspapers and Christmas supplements reported the experiences of the colonists for New Zealand readers, but the papers also travelled to Europe, where northerners regarded with some wonder the holiday experiences of their southern family and friends. Christmas cards, too, crossed the globe with increasing frequency in the late nineteenth century. Cheap postal rates encouraged the practice: it cost just a ha'penny to post a greeting card to Europe, a third of the cost of a postcard and a fifth of the postage for a letter.[78] Like the newspaper supplements, Christmas cards commonly portrayed the scenic beauties of the colony, as seen in the card produced by A. D. Willis of Wanganui, with its painting of one of the great wonders of New Zealand, the White Terraces, surrounded by that icon of a colonial Christmas, the pohutukawa flower.

An 1882 card by Saunders, McBeath & Co. of Dunedin also displayed scenic beauty surrounded by summer foliage and flowers, highlighting the portrayal of summer with the verse:

> Summer scenes and flowers, are ours at Christmas time,
> Not wint'ry frost and snow – as yours in Northern Clime.

The strange experience of a summer Christmas could not, however, completely divide the colonist from friends at home, and the verse continued:

> But still our hearts commingle, and kindly thoughts arise,
> Recalling distant lov'd ones who dwell 'neath other skies;
> And so I send this little gift across the ocean wide,
> Wishing 'A Glad New Year,' and 'A Merry Christmas-tide.'

The verse may have lacked literary merit but it did convey contemporary popular sentiments. As English historian Mark Connelly has argued, Christmas acted as 'a binding and integrating agent' of the British Empire, serving 'to create a sense of community and to remind the settlers of their motherland'. At the same time, by adapting to new surroundings Christmas celebrations in the colonies became 'an expression of nascent nationality'.[79] New Zealand Christmas cards and newspaper supplements demonstrated a powerful pride in the local alongside fond nostalgia for northern Christmases. They illustrated, for those at 'home', the exotic elements of a familiar celebration in the far reaches of the British Empire.

· ᴗ

One element of the Christmas celebrations significantly blended English tradition and colonial novelty: the food, which was a notable part of the festival. Communal feasting and drinking were central elements of the New Zealand Christmas in the early nineteenth century, but festive domestic meals became important in the celebrations of colonial families in later years. Families, which by the end of the century frequently extended to three or more generations in their new country, made a special effort to gather together for Christmas.

The Christmas meal generally included, where possible, the traditional English favourite, roast beef. Beef was not always easy to obtain in the early years of European settlement, and this made it a particularly special treat. On Christmas Day 1840, a group of settlers at Petone had 'a sumptuous feast of sucking pigs, pigeons, parakeets, sweet potatoes and fish' in the great outdoors. Best of all, though, 'some prime bullocks had been slaughtered for the occasion' so they enjoyed 'their share of beef – an unknown luxury in their little circle'.[80] Colonists in Christchurch were not so fortunate on their first Christmas, in 1850. Because of the heat and risk of spoilage, animals could not be slaughtered much in advance, and this led to a problem for one butcher, as Charlotte Godley explained: 'On Xmas Eve our butcher (for there are two!!) came to tell us that he had *lost* the bullock that was to have died for the Christmas dinners, and of which every joint was bespoke! He had driven it successfully towards home, having some miles to fetch it, but at two o'clock in the morning it had made its escape, and was not to be caught.'[81]

As farming became more established, beef became more readily available, some of it raised especially for the Christmas market. In 1850 one Wellington butcher obtained 'some of the finest Christmas beef supplied this year' in the form of four grass-fed oxen,

The Shakespear family of Little Barrier Island gathered for a Christmas feast, apparently in an awning or tent, around 1900. PHOTOGRAPH BY R. H. SHAKESPEAR, B4351, AUCKLAND WAR MEMORIAL MUSEUM LIBRARY.

Prime meats on display at David Taylor's butchery, Wadestown, Wellington, around the turn of the century. PHOTOGRAPH BY FREDERICK JAMES HALSE, G-10346-1/2, HALSE COLLECTION, ALEXANDER TURNBULL LIBRARY, WELLINGTON.

each weighing nearly 1000 pounds (450 kg), from Ngati Raukawa at Otaki, who used the profits to support their local Native Schools.[82] Butchers' special displays of meat soon became a feature of Christmas in every New Zealand town. The appearance of the Wellington butchers' shops on Christmas Eve 1862 was 'certainly gratifying in the extreme to all lovers of good cheer. Mighty carcases of slain oxen were there; sheep by dozens hung suspended for the inspection of foragers for the domestic commissariat, delicate lambs tempted the taste of the epicure, and dairy fed pork solicited the attention of lovers of bacon.'[83] Butchers competed with one another to present the largest beast, as in the 1800-pound (820 kg) cattle beast and 500-pound (230 kg) pig available for the Auckland Christmas market in 1872 (though, as the newspaper pointed out, discerning customers might be more interested in the quality than the quantity of the meat).[84]

For those who could not obtain beef, or preferred something different, other traditional favourites were available. In 1851, G. Edwards of Manners Street, Wellington, advertised '50 young geese for sale, Fatted expressly for Christmas Day'.[85] Fowl of all kinds proved popular, the *New Zealand Herald* commenting that 'the extensive purchases of poultry' on Christmas Eve 1888 showed 'the improved social condition of the people'.[86] Eating poultry was then a luxury, because birds were normally raised to lay eggs rather than for meat. The sight of specially fattened prime birds, ready to be killed for Christmas, proved too tempting for some residents of the Dunstan in 1868. Poultry disappeared mysteriously, and even the police fell victim to the thieves, for, as the newspaper reported, 'Mr Sub-Inspector Dalglish's fine fat goose, ordered for execution the following day, was amongst the missing ones'.[87]

Another old-world Christmas favourite, the plum pudding, was hugely popular in New Zealand. It assumed iconic significance for English colonists, featuring as the most recurrent image of Christmas in diaries, letters, reminiscences, newspaper reports, poems and stories. Boiled or steamed pudding was a particularly English creation: as one continental visitor to England declared in the seventeenth century, 'Blessed be he that invented pudding, for it is a manna that hits the palates of all sorts of people'. The plum pudding (plum, once referring only to the prune, became a generic term for dried fruit) was a delicious food readily available to all classes, for it required minimal fuel and ingredients.[88] In contrast with some other English Christmas traditions, ingredients for pudding were widely available, even in remote parts of the colony. One exception occurred at Raglan in 1883: residents were 'without raisins and currants for

Even those living in the most straitened circumstances made an effort to produce a special pudding at Christmas, as in the case of this gumdigger.
NEW ZEALAND OBSERVER AND FREE LANCE, 15 DECEMBER 1896, P. 7.

Christmas Day. The weather has been so bad that no steamer could come in . . . . If it does not abate, we shall fare very badly this festive season, as many of us are short of provisions.'[89]

In Lady Barker's 1872 tale of Christmas in rural New Zealand, old Bob, a shepherd, tells of his early days in the colony, when Christmas centred on the pudding:

As for Christmas Day, we never thought of it beyond wondering what sort of 'duff' we were going to have. That's colonial for a pudding, ma'am, you know, don't you? If we had a couple of handfuls of currants and raisins, we shoved them into a lot of flour and sugar,

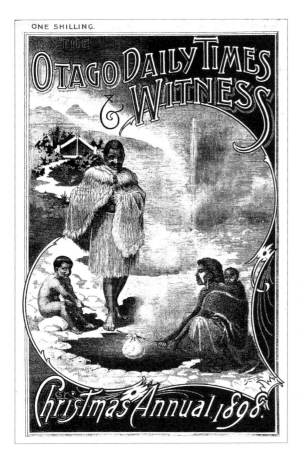

The illustration on the front of the popular *Otago Daily Times & Witness Christmas Annual* of 1898 demonstrated a distinctly New Zealand method of cooking the Christmas pudding: in a thermal pool. The portrayal – by Dunedin artist Robert Hawcridge – is probably imaginary, but conveys the sense of the exotic and the desire for the familiar felt by colonists at Christmas in their adopted country. It also reveals something of the way colonists felt an ideal Maori family would look – a nuclear group in front of an individual family home. OTAGO DAILY TIMES & WITNESS CHRISTMAS ANNUAL, 1898.

and we put a bit of mutton fat into the middle, and tied it all up together in the sleeve of an old flannel shirt and boiled it, and it used to come out a first-rate plum duff, and we thought we had had no end of a Christmas if we could manage such a pudding as that.[90]

The *New Zealand Observer and Free Lance*'s 1896 Christmas edition portrayed a gumdigger with his Christmas pudding in similarly spartan conditions. Other New Zealanders had the opportunity to cook pudding in a particularly colonial fashion: in 1884 the Washbourn family and friends, holidaying in the thermal regions of the Bay of Plenty, steamed their Christmas pudding in natural hot springs.[91]

Plain Plum Pudding.

½ lb. Flour	A grating of Nutmeg
½ lb. Breadcrumbs	1 saltspoon Salt
½ lb. chopped Suet	1 tablespoon Treacle
½ lb. Sultanas	1 teaspoon Spice
½ lb. Currants	2 Eggs
3 ozs. Peel	1 teaspoon Baking Powder
2 ozs. Sugar	½ cup Milk

Mix all the dry ingredients, add the eggs beaten,
and then the milk—just enough to moisten. Mix and
tie into a cloth dipped in boiling water and floured.
Drop into boiling water and boil four hours. Serve
with sweet sauce. If wanted richer, add one or two
eggs more, and less milk. It will be lighter if *no* sugar
is put in.

Old English Plum Pudding.

¼ lb. Breadcrumbs	1 teaspoon Spice
½ lb. Flour	1 saltspoon Salt
½ lb. Suet	1 oz. each Candied Peel
¼ lb. mashed Potatoes	and Citron
½ lb. boiled grated Carrot	¼ lb. Brown Sugar
¼ lb. Raisins	1 or 2 tablespoons Treacle
½ lb. Currants	

Mix with no other liquid than the treacle. Boil
four hours.

Vegetable Plum Pudding.

1 lb. mashed Potatoes	¾ lb. Brown Sugar
½ lb. mashed Carrots	½ lb. chopped Suet
1 lb. Flour	1 large teaspoon mixed
1 lb. Currants	Spice
1 lb. stoned Raisins	

Mix all thoroughly a fortnight before it is required.
No egg or no milk is wanted. Stir up every day.
Boil in a buttered mould five hours. This will keep a
long time. Re-boil when required.

A variety of recipes for the hugely popular plum
pudding from Elizabeth Brown Miller, a Dunedin
cookery teacher who began publishing her recipes
in the 1890s (this edition dates from 1904).
E. B. MILLER, *ECONOMIC TECHNICAL COOKERY BOOK*, MILLS
& DICK, DUNEDIN, 1904, P. 120.

Pudding even appeared in the midst of war. James Bodell, serving in the Waikato
Militia, spent Christmas 1863 at a small redoubt overlooking the Great South Road,
along with other militia men and soldiers from the 18th Regiment. On Christmas
Eve Mrs Martin, a local farmer's wife, gave Bodell the ingredients for a pudding and a
copper to boil it in. He and some mates then went on a daring (or, as they later realised,
foolish) night-time raid, hoping to purloin some poultry from a local farm for their
Christmas dinner. Their mission was unsuccessful, but 'Christmas day turned out
glorious, the large Plum Pudding was done to a turn having been kept boiling all Night,
and we passed a merry Christmas'.[92]

For most New Zealanders producing a plum pudding was straightforward.
Newspapers and cookbooks frequently included a recipe for this delicacy. For example,
the 1874 *Weekly News* Christmas supplement had four different recipes for plum
pudding. The first was huge, including two pounds each of suet, currants and raisins,

a pound of breadcrumbs, a pound and a half each of sugar and flour, half a pound of peel, fourteen eggs, half a pint of milk and some spices. The smallest version called for just half a pound each of suet, currants and raisins, along with very small quantities of flour, breadcrumbs and sugar, some spices, a little mild ale, and grated carrots and potatoes.[93] Dunedin cooking teacher Elizabeth Brown Miller's recipes for 'Old English Plum Pudding' and 'Vegetable Plum Pudding' also used root vegetables to keep the mixture moist and eke out the other ingredients.

Some family gatherings certainly called for large puddings, like the 16-pound (7 kg) monster Maria Atkinson made to feed the eighteen people present for Christmas dinner 1857 in her Taranaki home. The groaning table also featured beef, turkey, ham, fowl, almonds, raisins, Christmas mincemeat and gooseberry pie.[94] Dunedin bootmaker Jack Fowler received a huge pudding each year from his mother in London. As he wrote to her regarding a vintage effort in 1885, 'the only fault anyone says is that there is not enough of it for every one wanted a taste and few could say they have tasted its equal'. The following year he took his mother's pudding to a New Year's picnic, where 'there were at least 60 persons besides myself that had some of it'.[95] The pudding traffic went in both directions: Charles Collier of Auckland sent his mother in England a piece of his 1865 Christmas pudding.[96] Jack Fowler, however, returned his mother's generosity with a very colonial gift – a frozen lamb, timed to reach her in London just before Christmas.[97]

Roast beef and plum pudding would remain the most popular colonial Christmas dinner throughout the nineteenth century. 'No change of country or seasons', declared a Wellington newspaper, 'diminishes an Englishman's homage at this annual period of festivity, to plum-pudding and roast-beef, which are held in due honour in New Zealand'.[98] As Sarah Courage, the wife of a Canterbury runholder, remarked, 'our social habits are curiously obstinate; for under the heat-distilling skies of the Antipodes we wear much the same dress and we eat the same foods as in the frosty airs of the northern world'.[99] This custom reflected a strong commitment to a continuing English identity for many colonists; as a Wanganui newspaper correspondent noted in 1863, 'it requires some little nerve to look forward to roast beef and plum pudding, with the thermometer at 80 degrees [27 degrees centigrade]'.[100]

But the colonists also added new foods to their festive tables, prompted by their new living conditions. Thus their Christmas dinner is symbolic of their culture as a whole: they retained much-loved traditions from their old world, no matter how

Most New Zealanders enjoyed fresh summer vegetables, particularly new potatoes and peas, at Christmas dinner. Even urban dwellers could take pride in harvesting such vegetables from their own gardens, like this one in Berhampore, Wellington. Henry Wright photographed himself with son Reginald at their Britomart Street home in 1892.

G-66324-1/2, HENRY WRIGHT COLLECTION, ALEXANDER TURNBULL LIBRARY, WELLINGTON.

inappropriate they might be in their new environment, but also added elements of the new. They were proud of these colonial customs, describing them in detail for friends in Europe to wonder at. Among the treats for many New Zealanders were newly harvested vegetables which accompanied the traditional roast. Charles Collier boasted to his brother of the 'peas, new potatoes and cabbages' which he enjoyed on his first southern-hemisphere Christmas, while Vicesimus Lush wrote with some wonder in his diary, 'we had *green peas* and *new potatoes*, the first time I have partaken of them on a Xtmas Day'.[101] Summer fruits were another popular feature of the New Zealand Christmas. The *West Coast Times* raved about the wonderful produce available in Hokitika on Christmas Eve 1867 – one greengrocer displayed flowers, red currants, strawberries, cherries, 'first-class potatoes', cucumbers and 'gigantic lettuces'.[102] Strawberries were particularly favoured, and those who did not grow their own paid as much as two and a half shillings (half a day's wages for a labourer) per box in the Auckland Christmas market of 1893.[103] Aucklanders could also enjoy exotic tropical fruits – pineapples, bananas and oranges – imported from the Pacific Islands.[104]

New Zealanders generally indulged in summer fruit desserts as an addition to, rather than instead of, plum pudding. For Christmas 1873 the Lush family, who had been in New Zealand for over 20 years, enjoyed 'our usual orthodox dinner, roast beef and plum pudding and our New Zealand addition, cherry pie and custards'.[105] On his first colonial Christmas, at Wellington in 1850, builder Charles Carter 'dined off roasted goose, green peas, new potatoes, black currant (fresh gathered) pie, and, in memory of old England, we had as an extra, the *traditional plum pudding*'.[106] These detailed accounts of New Zealand Christmas dinners sent to family and friends in Europe symbolised not just the novelty of colonial life, but its abundance. This is most explicit in the letters of those who had left harsh conditions in their native land, such as agricultural labourer George Douch, who had struggled to make a living in his native Sussex but two years after his 1875 migration to Taranaki was building his own house on his own land. 'Never shall I forget', he wrote to his parents, 'the white plum pudding in 1855' (lacking fruit because of the family's poverty). In New Zealand, he would feast on 'new spuds and green peas, roast beef, and nine gallons of ale for this Christmas, that will be more like'.[107] The abundant New Zealand Christmas dinner was a symbol of success.

Some of the other Christmas foods we now consider 'traditional' were not so widespread in colonial New Zealand. Christmas cake – a rich fruit cake, elaborately decorated – emerged in late nineteenth-century England and was perhaps related to

Gathering strawberries, a popular Christmas treat, for the Auckland market. *AUCKLAND WEEKLY NEWS*, 12 JANUARY 1900, P. 7. S05-251B-E7016/24, HOCKEN COLLECTIONS, UARE TAOKA O HAKENA, UNIVERSITY OF OTAGO.

an earlier tradition of special cakes for Twelfth Night, which had once marked the end of the extended festivities of Christmas. As Helen Leach and Raelene Inglis's study of Christmas cakes in New Zealand suggests, fruit cake really began to gain popularity in the early twentieth century.[108] Nineteenth-century colonists could purchase special cakes from confectioners like Auckland's Charles Canning, who advertised a 'large variety of Christmas and twelfth-day cakes', which came plain, iced or ornamented.[109] The decorations on these cakes were rather different from those we might consider appropriate for Christmas today. Dallen, another Auckland confectioner, displayed for Christmas 1882 'a large number of Christmas cakes, iced with pretty bannerettes – the Royal Standard, the Union Jack, Stars and Stripes, &c., each bearing appropriate legends'.[110] But Christmas cakes and mince tarts, whether made at home or purchased from confectioners, were far less common and less significant than plum pudding and seldom received a mention in the colonists' letters and diaries. For Vicesimus Lush, cake was a poor substitute for pudding on his first colonial Christmas: 'there was not for us a Christmas pudding: we had to content ourselves with a plumb cake'.[111]

·

The Christmas tree is another feature, now taken for granted, dating from the late nineteenth century. Christmas decorations had been popular since colonisation began, with local greenery most readily accessible and widely used (though not yet in the form of a Christmas tree). In 1840, English settlers at Petone were still living in the most basic conditions, yet, as Brenda Northcroft Guthrie reports, at Christmas some of the young people 'made repeated excursions into the bush, coming back laden with tree ferns, ribbonwoods, misteltoe and greenery of all kinds. With long strips of flax they tied them all over the huts, inside and out, till my grandmother declared she couldn't get into hers for forest.'[112] Likewise, for Christmas 1893 a group of families busy clearing bush on their newly acquired sections in northern Wairoa decorated their 'faded whares . . . with new green leaves of the nikau and the great plumes of the mamaku'.[113] Some colonists found this use of the greenery which surrounded them in abundance rather ridiculous. 'It is curious', remarked an *Otago Witness* columnist, 'to note the reluctance of old customs to die, even though they have lost their reason of being. There is merit in greenery as a Christmas decoration when green things are scarce; little or none when nature is in her summer dress.'[114] Still the custom continued: the colonists clearly found great appeal in continuing the familiar European practice of adorning their homes and businesses for the season, just as they decorated their churches. This was something more than simple nostalgia, though, for they took pride in the New Zealand plants they used as decorations, just as they did in the summer fruit and vegetables which enhanced their Christmas dinners. Adopting aspects of the indigenous world in this way indicated a growing comfort with a once unfamiliar country: colonists were now becoming settled enough to appropriate native elements into their evolving culture.[115]

As the number of colonists grew, clearing ever more bush land, Christmas greenery became less accessible in expanding urban areas. In Auckland there was, the *Herald* reported in 1881, a 'growing scarcity' of the once popular tree-fern, nikau and pohutukawa 'in the vicinity of the town'.[116] The Domain had once supplied a ready

source of greenery, but that was now outlawed, although some Aucklanders still looked there in desperation: in 1879, five people received court summons 'for cutting down the tree ferns in the Domain, and six others for breaking the fences' in their hunt for decorations.[117] Perhaps more significant was that many Maori had left the district. They had once been the principal vendors of Christmas decorations, bringing bundles of toi toi, pohutukawa and ferns into town. Now that Maori no longer plied the trade, obtaining decorations required more trouble and expense for Auckland businesses.[118] Some city decorators thus began to turn to the artificial decorations which would become so popular in the twentieth century. In 1879 Abbott's United Service Hotel 'was elaborately displayed, the windows being set off with wax and gas lights, fringed with French artificial holly fronds and berries'.[119]

Real greenery remained, though, the first choice of Christmas decoration wherever possible. Flags were also popular. In the Otago goldmining town of Dunstan 'most of the hotels, shops, &c, were decorated with evergreens, and gaily colored flags floated over some of the buildings'.[120] Ships in harbour commonly displayed flags and bunting, but they made extra efforts at Christmas. At Auckland Harbour for Christmas 1876 'All the ships were dressed, from truck to taffrail . . . The English vessels were neatly decorated with the flags of many nations, while the coasters and local steamers, with the aid of ferns and evergreens, did their utmost to impart a novelty beyond the usual decorations incidental to shipping'.[121] Many businesses also featured special lighting displays for Christmas, often using the popular Chinese lantern. Jack Fowler described the scene at the Dunedin bootmaker's business where he worked in the 1880s: 'We had the usual decorations on the day before Xmas at the Shop big fern trees and evergreens all over the verandah and a big cartoon with A Merry Xmas on top and chinese lanterns hung about'.[122] It is difficult for us now, in a world ablaze with artificial light and neon signs, to appreciate the huge impact such displays had in the nineteenth century, when even regular street lights were few and far between. The effect must have been startling when British soldiers stationed at Te Awamutu during Christmas 1865 'metamorphosed the dreary old whares with bought and wonderful things in the shape of Chinese lanterns'.[123]

OPPOSITE: Greenery, particularly ferns, and summer flowers proved popular as colonial Christmas decorations. Women and children commonly planned and installed the decorations. *ILLUSTRATED NEW ZEALAND HERALD*, 17 JANUARY 1873, P. 6.

J. L. Williams's famous illustration of Queen Victoria, Prince Albert and their family at Windsor Castle with their Christmas tree helped spread the fashion for such trees in England and beyond. First published in the *Illustrated London News* Christmas Supplement, December 1848. N-P 1115-409, ALEXANDER TURNBULL LIBRARY, WELLINGTON.

Although Christmas greenery had been a common decoration for generations, the Christmas tree was unfamiliar to most mid-nineteenth-century Britons. Long popular in Germany, Holland and Scandinavia, Christmas trees came to Britain with German migrants, gradually spreading to the wider population. They started to become fashionable among the English middle classes after publicity about their use in the home of that most notable of German migrants, Prince Albert, in the 1840s.[124] In New Zealand, too, the domestic Christmas tree was most popular with German migrants, such as the small community at Upper Moutere. Anna Heine, daughter of the local Lutheran pastor, wrote in her diary of the Christmas trees which were one of the highlights of the season for their large family during the 1870s. They had trees both at church and home, sometimes lighting the candles that adorned them on several consecutive evenings. After her marriage to Lutheran missionary Hartwig Dierks, Anna lived at the Hermannsburg Mission Station at Waitotara, where the Christmas trees in her home and church delighted local Maori.[125]

Beyond the German community, Christmas trees were not particularly common as domestic items. Examples tend to come from wealthier homes, such as that of Wellington's Russell family, who in 1878 had a Christmas tree and 'a number of children for two hrs to see it on Xmas Eve', with 'a lot of pretty little presents for the various children'.[126] Most New Zealanders first encountered Christmas trees in institutions, notably in schools, Sunday schools and churches. Many a school end-of-year party featured a Christmas tree. At Waikaia, Southland, the most notable Christmas event in 1889 was 'the annual Christmas tree for the children', held at the school on Christmas Eve. 'The tree presented a brilliant spectacle, lit up with candles and Chinese lanterns, and bending beneath its valuable load of miscellaneous goods provided by the indulgent parents and friends of the little ones.'[127] Another typical end-of-year celebration was held at the Sunday school of St Matthew's Church, Auckland, in 1880, where 'the evening passed right merrily'. The main feature was a large Christmas tree, which 'blossomed with a good variety of nice things both ornamental and useful, things to play with, things to wear, things to eat, and things to admire in bountiful profusion'.[128]

The main function of a Christmas tree was to provide an attractive background for the display of gifts – toys, books, needlework and items of clothing, toiletries, sweets and fruit. The gifts hung on the branches of a pine tree, lit with either wax candles or Chinese lanterns. The highlight of any good 'Christmas tree entertainment' came with the distribution of the gifts (sometimes called prizes); frequently each child received a ticket whose number corresponded with a particular item on the tree. Some organisations, especially churches, used Christmas trees to raise funds, selling tickets for the gifts. In 1895 Mrs Knight's 'Christmas tree entertainment' raised funds for Dr Barnardo's home for destitute children in London. The grounds of the Knights' Ponsonby home 'were decorated with flags and bunting, and in the evening were lighted with Christmas lanterns, while the tree, ablaze with wax candles and loaded with all kinds of presents, presented a very pretty appearance. The youngsters were regaled with innumerable good things, and all obtained prizes.' About 120 children attended, presumably paying for their entrance.[129]

Other philanthropists used Christmas trees more directly to help the unfortunate. In 1872 the 65 children living at the Otago Benevolent Institution in Caversham attended a special Christmas Eve party provided by 'friendly donors'. After outdoor sports, the children were 'plentifully supplied with tea, fruit, and confectionery. They were then taken into a room in the building, which was decorated with evergreens and flowers, with two tall Christmas trees at one end'. Each child 'underwent the delightful operation of taking a ticket from a bag, and receiving something substantial'.[130] Some wealthy colonists in rural districts did not reserve their philanthropy for the needy, arranging Christmas treats for the whole neighbourhood. At their Garthmyl estate in the Strath Taieri, Otago, Alice and Edward Humphreys gave an annual midsummer picnic featuring a Christmas tree and abundant gifts for the whole neighbourhood. In keeping with the aristocratic style in which she had been raised in South Canterbury, 'at Christmas-time Mrs Humphreys visited all the families around, taking to them gifts of a side of bacon, vegetables and flowers'.[131]

Such seasonal bounty from the wealthy landowner to all those in the surrounding district was an old English custom that persisted only in isolated pockets of colonial New Zealand, which had a more egalitarian social structure. What did survive in the colonies was the practice of giving a Christmas gift (commonly called a Christmas 'box') to those who had provided a service during the year. Auckland newspaper columnist 'Mercutio' made a light-hearted complaint about the practice in 1888:

> Everybody who does anything about a man's house during the year expects to have a Christmas box. The postman has an ancient claim, of which we are reminded in the politest form possible; the dustman and the nightman will not admit that their claims are in any way inferior . . . . Still, we suppose that we mustn't be Scrooges, and must hope that a few shillings distributed to help the general rejoicing will bring good luck for the ensuing year, and tend to induce the more hopeful feeling we are all seeking to inspire.[132]

Simple philanthropy also remained a feature of Christmas. 'It is usual at Christmas time', declared the *New Zealand Herald* in 1873, 'for the kindly disposed to forward to the relief of the suffering and the poor, such donations in money or in kind as their liberality of spirit may suggest'. The practice would, declared the paper, 'bring a purer source of enjoyment to the donor than many days of selfishly indulged amusement'.[133] Christmas philanthropy often took the form of food or entertainment, but simple gifts also proved most acceptable to those dependent on charity. In 1872, for example, the 'inmates' of Auckland's Old Men's Refuge expressed their gratitude for the Christmas pudding provided by Mrs Beckham and a present of pipes, tobacco and matches from Mr J. Blair.[134] The prisoners in Dunedin Gaol were delighted with 'a quantity of beer' given by Mayor Thomas Birch, a wine merchant, as a Christmas treat in 1868.[135]

For most New Zealanders, Christmas gifts came from family and friends and were simple gifts of love or esteem. Their quality and quantity varied hugely according to individual family circumstances. Sarah Marsden Smith, who lived with her bank manager brother in comfortable circumstances in Dunedin, received various luxury items from family and friends for Christmas 1889: a bottle of eau de Cologne, vases, a photograph frame, a small toilet glass and volumes of Scott and Wordsworth.[136] Meanwhile, also in Dunedin, Mary Bailes, who made a living for her large family as a seamstress, scraped together a shilling each for her children to buy a toy, 'the only one in the year'. 'However did Mother spare that shilling?' her daughter Esther later wondered.[137] For Christmas 1893, the best that a group of struggling settlers clearing their new bush sections at northern Wairoa could manage was an even simpler gift: 'by dint of pinching and scraping just a bit more some brightly-coloured boiled lollies had been bought for the children'.[138]

Most colonists fell somewhere between these extremes of comfort and poverty. Many gave presents they had made themselves, and others could purchase such items from the fundraising bazaars often held just before Christmas. Anna Dierks, wife of a Lutheran missionary, put much time and effort into preparing gifts for Christmas. In November 1885, for example, she travelled from the Hermannsburg Mission to Wanganui to have her young daughter photographed. She then sent copies of the photograph to several family members as Christmas gifts. For others she used her needlework skills to make silk watch-chains, knitted scarves, bookmarks, collars and purses. Her young niece and god-daughter Johanne received 'a small apron with crewel outline and also a collar'; she made a small doll for her daughter; and 'for my dear husband I made a little watch-chain and tobacco pouch, for which he was real happy'.[139] These were certainly gifts of love.

Like Christmas cards, Christmas gifts could cross the world, helping maintain family ties despite the distance created by migration. Dunedin bootmaker Jack Fowler always received from his family in London a Christmas package containing a mix of practical items and special treats. In 1885 his English box contained a Christmas

Family photographs and images of local scenes were popular nineteenth-century Christmas and New Year gifts. In this 1898 advertising flyer, Port Chalmers photographer David De Maus offered photographs in a variety of sizes (including the small 'cabinet' size) and Christmas cards of local scenes 'suitable for sending home'. By today's standards, nineteenth-century advertising was rather plain, often featuring text alone. There were no holiday-themed pictorial images in the advertising in Victorian newspapers, which relied chiefly on different font sizes and styles for visual impact. MS-2462/029, GEORGE CRAIG THOMSON PAPERS, HOCKEN COLLECTIONS, UARE TAOKA O HAKENA, UNIVERSITY OF OTAGO.

pudding, two pairs of boots (walking and dress), slippers, a decorative pin, a bracket, views of the Exhibition, tobacco and cigars. He particularly appreciated the cigars: 'they were real good Cigars are very dear here 6d each and not very good at that so I generally do without them'. For some years he could send only cheap gifts, if any, in return – Christmas cards, for example – but as he became more prosperous he sent more substantial, though still far from extravagant, items to his distant family. In 1890 he sent his mother a small parcel containing photographic Christmas cards from the

Exhibition, a book of views, shells, a piece of greenstone found by his father-in-law at Moeraki, ferns, and a pincushion and watch pockets made by his wife, Jeannie.[140] These gifts, with their native New Zealand flavour, must have seemed exotic to a London family, besides conveying the affection of the far-distant Jack. Eliza Jones, struggling to cope with 'the excessive heat, the strange surroundings and the absence of familiar faces' on her second Christmas in New Zealand, in 1858, found comfort in gifts from her loved ones: 'the kindly gifts I received reminded me that loving hearts had me in remembrance still and I shall always value the handsomely bound book for ferns which dear Humphrey [her brother] and Emma gave me'.[141]

For most nineteenth-century New Zealanders, Christmas presents came by simple gift exchange or, occasionally, from a Christmas tree. By the end of the century, though, a new form of gift delivery had arrived – the stocking filled by Santa Claus. In Britain, Christmas had been personified – as were many seasons and festivals – since the seventeenth century, taking the form of an old man with flowing beard, frequently known as Father Christmas. He represented feasting and frolics but had no specific function other than as a figure of fun.[142] The personification of Christmas as an old man seemed rather incongruous to some nineteenth-century New Zealanders, but many continued to refer to the coming of the season in the personal form of 'old Christmas' or 'Father Christmas'.

In the middle of the century a more developed personification of Christmas arrived in England from Europe via the United States of America. Dutch children looked forward to a visit from St Nicholas, or Santa Claus, on St Nicholas Eve (5 December), when the kindly saint left them gifts, provided they had been good. Dutch migrants brought the custom with them to America, where it moved to Christmas Eve and became common in the wider community. Clement Clarke Moore's poem 'A Visit from St Nicholas' (better known by its first line, ''Twas the night before Christmas . . .') and Thomas Nast's illustrations for *Harper's Weekly* were hugely influential in creating the image of Santa Claus so familiar today: a jolly old man in a red suit lined with white fur, who travelled in a sleigh drawn by reindeer, arrived via the chimney and left presents for children in their stockings. This new Santa became popular in England from the 1870s and 1880s onwards, although he usually took the old name of Father Christmas and wore a hood rather than the American cap.[143]

From the late 1860s New Zealand children and parents could learn about the Father Christmas custom in their local newspapers. The *Otago Witness*, for example, printed

Mabel and Ellen check their Christmas bounty, from the story 'Christmas Stockings' in a local school reader. The blazing fire in the background suggests that this image may have come originally from a northern-hemisphere source. THE IMPERIAL READERS (SOUTHERN CROSS SERIES), THIRD READER, WHITCOMBE & TOMBS, WELLINGTON, CHRISTCHURCH AND DUNEDIN, [1899], P. 43.

the poem 'A Visit from St Nicholas' on Boxing Day 1868, and their Christmas features in the years 1876 to 1879 carried poems or stories about Santa Claus.[144] By the 1880s, reports on Christmas shopping commonly referred to parents' work on behalf of the jolly saint, as on Christmas Eve 1888 in Auckland, where 'the toy emporiums were crowded to excess with devoted parents, who had entered into league with Santa Claus'.[145] Even the Catholic newspaper, the *New Zealand Tablet*, made its contribution, noting in 1884 that 'little children, with the faith of childhood, are dreaming of their good friend Santa Claus, that ever-living beneficent fairy who came to us in our childish days, and who is still willing to delight our little ones by filling their stockings from his ample stores'.[146]

School reading books formed another very important source of information for children, who often had to memorise the poems and stories in them. The *Imperial Readers*, published locally from 1899 by Whitcombe & Tombs as part of their Southern Cross series, included numerous references to Christmas. The first reader included the poem 'Hang up Baby's Stocking', where a young girl suggested her mother hang up grandma's longest stocking for the baby, as his own was far too small. She left a note for Santa Claus, ending 'Please cram this stocking with presents, from the top of it down to the toe'.[147] The story 'Christmas Stockings' in the third reader, published for slightly older children, had young Mabel and Ellen rising excitedly at dawn to check their stockings, where they found grapes, sugar-plums, gloves, a ball, pincushions embroidered with their initials, Cologne, raisins and almonds. One of the most intriguing aspects of this story is that it has no mention of Santa Claus or Father Christmas – instead the girls discuss which friend or relative has given each gift in the stocking.[148] Were the children now too old for the Santa myth? Perhaps the story simply reflects the novelty of Christmas stockings. Many nineteenth-century New Zealanders may have lacked enthusiasm for maintaining the fiction of the 'ever-living beneficent fairy' for their children, and no doubt some opposed such pretence outright.

For those whose parents did enter into the new practice, Christmas was certainly a time of great excitement. Ellen Windsor of Napier recalled the Christmases of her 1890s childhood:

> we always hung our stockings (strong black woollen stockings we always wore) from the kitchen mantelpiece, and what joy in the morning when we discovered what Santa Clause [*sic*] had left us – always an orange and any other fruit available, some nuts, a tiny penny packet of sweets and some little novelty, and perhaps a handkerchief, a ball, or a china mug, a little doll, and always a book.

The gifts were, as she notes, 'very simple by today's standards but we were well content and so happy with everything'.[149] And many of us can relate to William Mills's description of Christmas spent with friends, the large Montgomerie family, near Marton in 1883:

A youthful Santa Claus guides Hal and Cis on their magical tour in Kate McCosh Clark's children's book, which attempted to promote Christmas trappings appropriate for the summer season. ILLUSTRATION BY R. ATKINSON IN KATE MCCOSH CLARK, *A SOUTHERN CROSS FAIRY TALE*, SAMPSON LOW, MARSTON, SEARLE & RIVINGTON, LONDON, 1891. B-K 448-6/7, ALEXANDER TURNBULL LIBRARY, WELLINGTON.

On Xmas Eve Mrs M[ontgomerie] & I filled all the childrens stocking with toys & lollies (goodies at Home). You may imagine the excitement in the morning, but you cannot imagine the infernal (there's no other word, Mother) row, 2 squeaky dolls & three horns, one with a row of pipes, all hard at it in the early hours.[150]

Occasionally Father Christmas appeared in person, usually at Christmas tree entertainments. In 1888 he 'put in an appearance amidst shouts of laughter' at the 'Christmas tree and bazaar' held to raise funds for the Anglican church at Tuakau, south of Pukekohe.[151] As the century drew to a close, a new opportunity arose for New Zealand children to meet Santa in the flesh. In December 1894 Wellington department store the D.I.C. announced that 'Old Father Christmas, with his Christmas Tree and thousands of Toys for Boys and Girls' would arrive in store. 'His gigantic Christmas Tree and his thousands of Toys will be found in the D.I.C. Furniture Room.'[152] The

'Young New Zealand's welcome to Santa Claus' portrays the mythic figure in the style which came to pervade popular culture. Santa may have been an import, but a Maori girl, complete with moko and mere, accompanies the confident Pakeha boy addressing the visitor. From the cover of the *Auckland Weekly News* Christmas Supplement, 1887. N-P III6-SUPPL-I, ALEXANDER TURNBULL LIBRARY, WELLINGTON.

practice, imported from overseas, moved to department stores in other New Zealand towns in the early twentieth century. Soon Father Christmas began arriving with great fanfare into increasingly ornate 'magic caves'; Santa parades drew the crowds; and, by the 1920s, 'Santa's presence was well established as an annual institution in the toy section of New Zealand department stores'.[153]

In the nineteenth century, though, Santa Claus remained something of a novelty, and some New Zealanders still felt the old man dressed in fur did not belong to a summer Christmas. Kate McCosh Clark's *Southern Cross Fairy Tale*, a fantasy for children published in 1891, tells the tale of young Hal and Cis, who are taken on a magical Christmas Eve tour of New Zealand's natural wonders and beauties by Santa Claus. When Hal and Cis are first woken by Santa they do not recognise him, for he is 'a lad with a smiling face, and on his head was a crown of twinkling stars'. When he finds out who the mysterious visitor is, Hal declares 'Why, I thought Santa Claus was an old man', only to receive the reply, 'So I am, in the Old World . . . but here, in the New World, I am young likc it'.[154] But attempts like Clark's made little progress: the fat old man in the winter suit was a hugely powerful icon; he captured the public imagination and proved irresistible as the personification of Christmas.

·⤸

As Christmas grew in popularity it became, for some, a two-day holiday. Boxing Day (so called because it was the customary day for giving a Christmas 'box' or gift to servants and tradesmen) had once been part of the extended medieval Christmas and New Year festival, but the 26 December holiday faded, along with the rest, until its resurrection as a popular addition to Christmas in the Victorian period.[155] English migrants brought the custom to New Zealand, where other residents viewed it as a particularly *English* custom – it was 'the English Carnival' or 'the true English Saturnalia', declared the *New Zealand Herald*.[156] Charles Collier, an English migrant working in an Auckland engineering shop, explained to his brother that he did not have a holiday for Boxing Day: 'my employer is a scotch man and he only stopped on Christmas day but at the new year there was a stoppage of 2 days so that you see that with a great many people the new year is the grand day'.[157] Although Boxing Day did not catch on with all New Zealand residents, it grew in prevalence until it became, by the early twentieth century, an accepted part of the holiday calendar. It provided an opportunity for outdoor recreation, with the excursions, picnics, races and sports typical of nineteenth-century holidays. But it was on the 'grand day', New Year, that outdoor activities were to prove most popular.

By the turn of the century Christmas was a different occasion from the riotous feast or the sober and serious religious service which had marked the festival in the earliest years of European settlement in these islands. With growing migration, the establishment of more and more families, and the rise of the middle class and 'respectable' working class, it became a holiday increasingly centred on the family and the younger generation. The increasing significance of the child and the family at Christmas was not, however, peculiar to New Zealand, but a broad international trend, epitomised in two late nineteenth-century innovations: the Christmas tree and Santa Claus. These new, child-focused Christmas traditions also reflected the growth

A group of young Dunedinites ham it up for the camera on a Boxing Day picnic, around 1897.

of modern consumer culture, for both featured Christmas gifts. We should be wary, though, of idealising a more innocent, less commercialised past era of holidays, for they have always included a business element. In 1849, J. Fraser of Wellington advertised 'a great variety of Toys, suitable for Christmas presents or New Years Gifts', while R. J. Duncan offered 'wines and spirits of the *best* quality at the *lowest* prices' for 'Christmas and the New Year Holidays'.[158] Christmas marketing would become more prevalent and extend for ever greater periods in later decades, but it was not new; as American historian Leigh Schmidt points out, complaining about the commercialisation of the holidays is itself an old holiday tradition.[159]

The religious traditions of Christmas also changed over the nineteenth century. Christmas services became more festive, with an ever-increasing abundance of

Some of the crowd at the New Plymouth summer race meeting, Boxing Day 1899. FROM *AUCKLAND WEEKLY NEWS*, 5 JANUARY 1900, P. 4. S05-251A-E7016/23, HOCKEN COLLECTIONS, UARE TAOKA O HAKENA, UNIVERSITY OF OTAGO.

decorations and carols. Those denominations that had once frowned upon such frivolities began to have second thoughts about their disapproval of the feast of the nativity, and Christmas became a spiritual occasion for a larger proportion of New Zealanders in the twentieth century. The religious and secular traditions evolved alongside one another and remained significant in the lives of many residents. Both responded to the environmental conditions of the south while retaining traditions of the north: churchgoers sang English carols but decorated their buildings with pohutukawa and ferns; families feasted on roast beef and plum pudding but accompanied them with new vegetables and summer fruit. Christmas was a reflection of New Zealand's nineteenth-century culture: a blend of the old and the new, the indigenous and the imported; a mixture of religion and revelry, family and community.

᷒

CHAPTER TWO

New Year

By almost any measure – time spent in preparation, degree of anticipation, media hype, money spent, food consumed, complexity of ritual involved, stress created – Christmas is now New Zealand's greatest holiday. That was not the case in the nineteenth century, when New Year took the prize as the colony's greatest regular celebration. Scottish migrants, many of them with little regard for Christmas, preferred to save their energies for 1 January, the great Scottish holiday. As the *Otago Witness* declared in 1864, 'The Otagans have now, it may be said, fixedly set apart New Year's Day as their high holiday'.[1] Those businesses which tried to carry on as usual on New Year's Day sometimes gave up the effort in response to community enthusiasm for the holiday. Those who made the attempt in Dunedin in 1865 'found the holiday spirit too strong for them', reported the newspaper. 'By noon, every warehouse and almost every shop was closed for the day.'[2]

But the Scots did not confine their influence to the south. Wherever they were, they celebrated New Year with enthusiasm and, as there were at least a few Scots in most colonial communities, others were quickly exposed to their customs. The convivial and enjoyable Scottish New Year traditions clearly held so much appeal that others happily adopted them. New Year 'takes precedence of Christmas', declared an Auckland paper in 1874, 'as one section of the community refuse to give the observance to that day which they cheerfully accord to the 1st of January'.[3] In the 1880s a newspaper noted New Year as 'the chief holiday of the year. It is in fact everybody's holiday.'[4]

The New Year holiday could be readily adopted by most New Zealanders because there was little in it to cause offence. The *New Zealand Herald* explained in 1879:

Its celebration as a festival is neither confined to creeds nor parties . . . . The day will be, in every sense of the word, a day of recreation. Unlike Christmas Day, it is not, so to speak, a religious festival, and persons entering on the enjoyment of rational sports will not be looked upon by their pious neighbours as little better than desecrators of the Sabbath. In fact, the people may enjoy themselves, untrammelled by any restraints other than moral conduct, cordiality, and good feeling.[5]

Of course some people did not approve the rowdier goings-on of New Year's Eve, but they had the option of spending the time in quiet reflection, perhaps at one of the watch night church services, which came out of the English tradition and continued as a New Year's Eve activity in New Zealand.

One of the most intriguing features of the colonial New Year is not its similarity to the Scottish holiday but the differences that arose in the New Zealand setting. For Scottish migrants, a summer New Year was as striking as a summer Christmas to the English and Irish. Surveyor James McKerrow recalled his first colonial New Year in 1860:

warm night sunshine and strawberries and cream are very nice but for a New Year's day I could not help thinking they were a poor substitute for the dark night with the hail battering on the windows, the snug warm cosy room, the bright cheerful fire, the re-union of friends around the table, the crisp oat cakes and ham, the buttered toast, the currant bun and the other fine things that make up a good scotch tea.

An old friend, 'who did not feel quite at home amid the novelties of Colonial life', summed up this strange feeling for McKerrow when she commented that 'everything here is contrairy – for the south wind is cauld, the north wind is warm and the very sun, himsel gangs the wrang way about'.[6] Such comments on the 'upside-down' nature of colonial life should not be quickly dismissed. For migrants from the northern to southern hemispheres the topsy-turvy holiday was a poignant reminder of their former life and of the strangeness and novelty of their new social and physical environment. They were powerfully aware, at such times, that New Zealand was something more than just another Britain.

For some, midsummer seemed an inappropriate time to mark the New Year. 'It is part of the general upside-downedness of affairs in this hemisphere', remarked an

Otago Witness columnist, 'that the Old Year dies when Nature is fullest of lusty life. No people with any feeling for the poetic fitness of things would make the annual cycle end at midsummer. The years should die when the days are shortest, the trees leafless, the fields and gardens bare, all the vital forces of the natural world at zero.'[7] There is, of course, much merit in this argument. As people of the southern hemisphere, Maori traditionally celebrated the turning of the year with Matariki, in winter. For many Maori, the sign of the new year was the rising of the star cluster Matariki (the Pleiades) in the eastern dawn sky; some (including Nga Puhi and some Ngai Tahu hapu) instead looked to the reappearance of Puanga (Rigel) as the morning star, which occurs around the same time. Matariki was important as a signal to plant crops, but it was also a time to celebrate, to remember the year that had gone and those people who had died and to look for omens for the year ahead. These traditions came close to dying out, but the Maori cultural renaissance has seen their recent revival, and discussion of adding Matariki to the public holiday calendar.[8] The growing popularity of Matariki reflects the increasing desire of some New Zealanders to mark the southern seasons, seen also in the late twentieth-century development of midwinter or winter solstice celebrations (sometimes referred to as 'midwinter Christmas').[9]

Nineteenth-century migrants from Europe, though, had no interest in changing the times of their seasonal holidays or adopting Maori practice. They clung to their familiar calendar and marked the turning of the year on 1 January, a date their ancestors had recognised since the days of the Roman Empire and the festival of the Kalendae.[10] In their new home, though, the New Year festival had a very different feel.

·❥

In many New Zealand settlements the new year arrived, literally, with a bang. The fledgling community of Wellington welcomed 1841 with guns and bells, and 'the harbour, for some time, echoed with the roar of cannon and the mingled cheers of those who were determined to pay a mark of respect to the old year'.[11] In some districts the Volunteers – the local militia – took the opportunity to demonstrate their skills with firearms. In Invercargill, for example, New Year 1876 began 'with a salvo of artillery by the Volunteers under the command of Captain Heywood'.[12] Most large settlements had at least one cannon they could fire, and so did ships in the harbour. Those without ships

A 'very early' brass band in Alexandra. In many districts, local and military bands enlivened holiday celebrations with their music. Bands commonly 'played out the old year and played in the new' with 'Auld Lang Syne'. S06-518C-E1298/33, HOCKEN COLLECTIONS, UARE TAOKA O HAKENA, UNIVERSITY OF OTAGO.

or large guns simply fired smaller arms, as in the small West Otago farming community of Kelso in 1882, where 'just as the clock struck 12 shooting was heard in all directions, and all sorts of musical instruments were brought into requisition'.[13]

Recent English migrants could be startled by these unfamiliar celebrations. Frederick Haslam, attending the watch night service at the Congregational Church in Albert Street, Auckland, as 1864 commenced, wrote that 'at 12 o'clock fireworks were let off from the Ships in harbour and everybody nearly letting off their rifles in the streets. It was like a night attack and everyone asking to know what was the matter'.[14] The goldfields were particularly noisy places at New Year. At the Dunstan, at New Year 1864, the 'wee hours of morning were ushered in by rather uproarious demonstrations of joy in the shape of a band, consisting of some forty or fifty persons who formed a sort of musical or rather unmusical society led by a big drum . . . a flute and accordion, together with several bells, tin dishes and other noisy contrivances'.[15] During the 1870s, as kerosene lamps became increasingly available, a new instrument added to the New Year racket – the kerosene tin. The noises at New Year 1879 at Wanganui included bells, guns, shouting revellers and a 'band of youths making night hideous with kerosene tins'.[16]

Most settlements managed something a little more sophisticated in the way of music to 'play out the old year and play in the new', in the common expression of the day. Even isolated rural residents could sometimes enjoy the sounds of a band playing out the year. Those living in Patumahoe and the Mauku district, near Pukekohe, had an unexpected treat at New Year 1871. The Forest Rifle Volunteer Band paraded through the area and many 'were awakened from a sound sleep by this agreeable surprise'. The band received some reward for their efforts, being 'bountifully supplied with wine by Major Lusk, J.P., and also with a good substantial repast in the shape of coffee, and bread and butter, by Mr Mowbray'.[17]

In larger towns, the New Year's Eve crowds could enjoy the performances of several different bands. In Auckland, those thronging Queen Street on the last night of 1875 heard the music of the Thames Naval Brigade Band, the Temperance Band and the Hobson Band. In addition, 'several vocalists passed through the thoroughfares and delighted the pedestrians much by their fine rendering of glees. The strains of the concertina and flute were distinguishable almost everywhere, and numbers of people, unable to procure a suitable musical instrument, turned their voices to account by whistling in a vigorous manner.'[18]

At Stratford, the old year 1894 'died to the tune of "After the Ball," that mournful air being chosen as a requiem by the Brass Band'.[19] In playing this 'requiem' they broke with popular tradition, for almost every other musician in the country would have been playing 'Auld Lang Syne'. Robbie Burns had amended and enlarged this traditional Scottish song in the late eighteenth century, and his touch of genius and eventual worldwide fame gave it lasting popularity. It is appropriate that the world's most popular New Year anthem should come from the country whose New Year customs spread far and wide. Its use of Scottish language, though, renders the song obscure to many, and as Burns scholar Maurice Lindsay notes, 'it has aptly been described as "the song that nobody knows"', although plenty attempt to sing it.[20]

To New Zealand's nineteenth-century Scottish migrants the words, which refer to the reunion of two childhood friends, would have been readily understood. No doubt many shed a tear as they sang the line 'but seas between us braid [broad] hae roar'd', recalling their loved ones far away.[21] The soldiers of Britain's 40th and 65th Regiments,

Ships at Port Chalmers, near Dunedin, in December 1874. Those still in port at the end of the month would illuminate the New Year sky with an impressive display of lights and rockets. S06-518A-E2674/19, HOCKEN COLLECTIONS, UARE TAOKA O HAKENA, UNIVERSITY OF OTAGO.

stationed at Te Awamutu as 1865 began, certainly found the song moving. As 'the old year was about to pass away' the bands of these two regiments (which hailed from Somerset and Yorkshire) together played 'the old and appropriate air of "Auld Lang Syne"' in 'memory of our comrades who fell during the past year . . . . As this popular air was played, many a silent tear could be seen coursing down the veteran cheeks of officers and men as they thought of those who on last Christmas were amongst us, and who are now no more.'[22]

Most settlements had plenty of distractions to help ease any sorrow New Year's revellers may have felt as one year passed into another. Besides the multitude of noises, fireworks abounded. Often the best displays of fireworks came from ships in harbour. Ships carried fireworks – rockets, available in at least three colours (white, red and green), and 'blue lights' – so that they could give long-distance signals at sea.[23] They seem to have been happy enough, when in port, to use them in celebrations, especially

78

at New Year. The small town of Picton, for example, saw 'great rejoicing' at New Year 1890, when Captain Forsdick of the *Waipa* 'delighted the good people of the town and district by an exhibition of fireworks, blue lights, rockets, etc., from his vessel'.[24] In busier ports, ships competed with one another to produce the best display. Port Chalmers revellers witnessed a stunning show from the vessels in port at New Year 1879. The steamer *Albion* 'opened the ball by burning blue lights on each yard arm, sending up a magnificent display of rockets, firing a royal salute, and continuously ringing her bell'. Other ships followed suit, with the barque *Mataura* 'especially noticeable in her display, seamen being stationed on her yard arms burning coloured lights at appropriate intervals, while a brilliant display of rockets were sent up, and a due amount of guns fired by her crew'.[25]

Such displays made the port the obvious spot for New Year's Eve revellers to gather in many towns. New Year was a subdued occasion in English- and Irish-dominated Christchurch, and those who preferred a more exuberant style of celebration learned to make the trip to Lyttelton. There, in 1868, the 'town was alive with people, many going to Sticking Point to see the ships which are generally lighted up on this occasion'. At midnight they heard the sounds of the ships' bells and watched the 'splendid lights' from the ships in port. Meanwhile, 'several singing parties patrolled the town, and it was not until daybreak that the proceedings ceased'.[26] In Auckland, the Queen Street wharf was always at the centre of the evening's liveliest activity. This was the best spot to see the fireworks, hear the bands and join the singing and dancing, as in 1881 when, soon after 12 o'clock,

> the Naval Band marched down the wharf, halting on the tee. This proved an excel-
> lent opportunity for the youths with life and mettle on their heels, and soon dozens of
> them were vigorously whirling around in the polka, schottische, or mazy waltz, with
> bearded partners, to the music of the band. Numerous frolicsome lads and young men,
> wearing hideous masks or false faces, mingled with the crowd.[27]

Women were also present, but apparently felt less need than did the young men to relieve themselves 'of their surplus energy and good spirits'. The Queen Street wharf did have its disadvantages as a gathering place: those who had been imbibing freely could fall off and drownings were not unknown. Another option was to watch the events from one of the popular moonlight harbour excursions.[28]

Auckland's Queen Street wharf, photographed in October 1883. This was the city's most popular New Year's Eve gathering place. Revellers sang and danced on the wharf, and a few fell into the harbour.
PHOTOGRAPH BY JAMES D. RICHARDSON, 4-561, SPECIAL COLLECTIONS, AUCKLAND CITY LIBRARIES.

From the 1870s, other rockets began to join those fired from ships in the New Year's Eve sky. In Auckland, at midnight on the last day of 1878, 'almost simultaneously were seen issuing from the heights of Mounts Eden, Albert, Hobson, and One-tree Hill, a brilliant display of fireworks, which lighted up the localities as if a shower of meteors were descending'. The display had been arranged by a 'party of gentlemen' to offer 'congratulations and wishes for a happy New Year to each and all'.[29] Few displays reached this level of co-ordinated sophistication, although midnight could find fireworks blazing from different locations around a town, as at Lyttelton at New Year 1880. Residents in various parts of the town discharged fireworks 'with a bountiful hand, and the effect produced was one of the finest ever seen, the various colours illuminating the buildings and back-ground of the hills magnificently'.[30] Businesses, notably hotels, sometimes joined in with the pyrotechnics, as at Port Chalmers in 1883, when the Port Chalmers, Marine, and George Hotels gave 'a splendid display of rockets and coloured fires, the Port Chalmers Hotel in addition sending up a great number of coloured fire-balloons'.[31]

In some districts the local fire brigade found New Year's Eve an ideal time to hold processions and give fireworks displays. The residents of New Plymouth, Timaru and Hokitika, for example, all had the opportunity to witness such demonstrations during the 1890s.[32] In the mining town of Reefton, welcoming in 1896, the fire brigade's usual display also turned into an opportunity to practise their fire-fighting skills when 'all the rockets, candles, etc., exploded together and set the manual engine on fire. One member of the Fire Brigade got his hand badly burnt through the mishap'.[33]

Fortunately, such accidents seem to have been rare, but this can hardly be attributed to sensible behaviour – New Year revellers often discharged fireworks with reckless disregard for public safety. In 1875 the crowds parading the main streets of Dunedin fired rockets and threw bundles of crackers 'in every direction', including at passing vehicles. 'A constant discharge of crackers and even of rockets was kept up against the upstairs windows of Dunning's, those in the Café returning the compliment by throwing crackers in the crowd below and discharging rockets.' Local by-laws forbade such behaviour, but the vastly outnumbered police could only 'look quietly on – it would have taken a very big lock-up to hold all who let off fireworks last evening, or a great many policemen to take down their names'.[34]

The 'cracker nuisance' continued throughout the century. These devices (along with their close relative the 'squib', which hisses before it explodes) were cheap, readily available, and evidently much beloved by boys young and old. In 1891, New Zealanders imported £753 worth of fireworks. No doubt crackers and squibs made up a substantial proportion of these imports. About half of New Zealand's fireworks came from Hong Kong, reflecting their popularity and significance for Chinese migrants, who used them in many ceremonies. But fireworks also came to New Zealand from the United Kingdom and Australia, and could be purchased in European as well as Chinese stores.[35] The Auckland police had more success than their Dunedin colleagues in keeping the New Year fireworks under control. On New Year's Eve 1889 the *Herald* announced that the police had 'strict instructions to prosecute any persons letting off crackers or discharging fireworks in the streets this evening'. This proved to have 'a dispiriting effect on the local pyrotechnists' and the 'display of fireworks was scarcely up to that of previous years'.[36]

ABOVE AND OPPOSITE: New Year's Eve 1899 in the public and saloon bars of the Café de Paris, Cashel Street, Christchurch. Apart from the barmaids, this was clearly a man's world. Note the festive decorations. *WEEKLY PRESS*, 10 JANUARY 1900, P. 70. 1923.53.461 AND 1923.53.462, BISHOP COLLECTION, CANTERBURY MUSEUM.

The New Year's Eve revellers who crowded the streets of many towns were not all young and rowdy. As the *Otago Witness* noted in 1879, those joining the celebrations in Dunedin included 'a number of douce and sensible citizens, many of them with their wives and even families', wandering the streets 'to see what was to be seen and to welcome the coming of the New Year'.[37] New Year high spirits were, in many cases, fuelled to a large extent by alcohol. In 1850, Reverend Thomas Burns of Dunedin reported that New Year's Eve featured not just noise, but drunkenness 'on the part of some few of our people'.[38] Such behaviour continued throughout the century. In 1873

a columnist noted that the large quantities of spirits recently reported to be in storage in Dunedin must have been 'considerably reduced by the New Year festivities'. The resulting 'joviality . . . extended to all classes . . . some of the "nobs" . . . were quite as "happy" as the Messrs Brogden's navvies, who gave ample public evidence that they were not teetotallers'.[39] Some drank in the streets, like those 1878 Dunedin revellers who observed 'the time honoured custom of parading the streets with bottles of whisky in their hands, and forcing their friends to drink to the New Year'.[40] Others crowded the local pubs, some of which offered free drinks as the clock struck midnight.

This time-honoured custom could be seen, for example, at Arrowtown in 1899, where the hotels 'enlivened' the New Year proceedings by keeping 'free house, dispensing champagne, wines, whisky and all other liquors "free, gratis, for nothing," at 12 o'clock, as the old year departs'.[41]

The extent of New Year's Eve drinking – or at least of drunkenness – seems to have varied greatly from year to year. In 1874, for example, an Auckland paper reported that the crowds of revellers were 'bent upon enjoying themselves in moderation. There was a total absence of that drunkenness which was oftentimes so conspicuous here on similar occasions several years ago.'[42] As temperance sentiment grew towards the end of the century, some began to take another look at their New Year customs. At Woodside, on the Taieri, those gathered at an 1880 New Year's Eve party arranged by the Good Templars toasted one another at midnight with 'fragrant congou' (tea) rather than the more traditional whisky.[43] But alcohol remained the New Year's toast of choice for many throughout the century, and the 'customary number of festive souls' could still be 'met at every corner' of Dunedin's main street on New Year's Eve 1896, just as the customary number of people appeared in Magistrates' Courts throughout the country on the customary New Year's charge of drunkenness.[44]

· ◡

Many people, of course, saw the New Year in at home, with friends or at community gatherings rather than on the street or in the pub. In 1897 the society column of the *Otago Witness* reported 'the usual family gatherings, which are annual events in many of the old-established households of Dunedin', on New Year's Eve. Although 'many amused themselves in the usual manner by "doing the town" during the evening, by midnight the greater number had retired to the warmth and shelter of their own homes or to "first-foot" the homes of some of their acquaintances'.[45] One such 'old-established household' would have been that of Sarah Marsden Smith, who lived with her bank manager brother and his family and was active in social and philanthropic circles. In the early hours of 1890 she wrote in her diary: 'We have just finished a very pleasant evening. J & E Salmond, Jessie Hall, M & A Kirkland, P & M Dunlop, Mr Gilkison and ourselves. We saw the old year out and now have entered on the New.'[46] Those in humbler circumstances also enjoyed gatherings with friends and neighbours on 31 December. Young carpenter William Turnbull Smith, a new arrival in the colony, saw in the New Year of 1864 with his neighbours and fellow Scots, the Smaill family of Inchclutha (South Otago). After tea 'the party retired into the barn where dancing was continued till the dawn of day 1864'.[47] Also dancing in the New Year were some residents of Kaiapoi, who in 1870 'seemed to thoroughly enjoy themselves in carrying out the Scotch custom of dancing "the old year out and the new year in"' at a 'grand Caledonian Ball'.[48]

For many Scottish and northern English migrants, New Year would not be complete without a visit from 'first footers'. Tradition held that the type of first foot – the first person to cross the threshold in the new year – determined the luck of the household for the rest of the year. Those considered most lucky varied from district to district, but many believed that a dark-haired man, bearing whisky and maybe a symbol of food for the table and fuel for the hearth, was the best of first footers.[49] Charles Hayward, originally from Suffolk, who had married into a Scottish family in the Catlins district of South Otago, described in his 1866 diary what was to him an unfamiliar practice:

> Robt & I were out early this morning, to take the round of the Flat to wish them all a happy New Year, this though not practised in England, is the regular custom in Scotland, and is called the first footing. The person calling must manage to be at the house or houses at which he intends to call as early as possible to prevent being fore-stalled by any one else, and he is also supposed to take with him a bottle of spirits and a piece of cake, and to help every one in the house to the same, and any one refusing to take of the offering it is considered an insult, and of course is never done without such an intention.[50]

It is difficult to determine how common the practice was in New Zealand. In 1893 the *N.Z. Presbyterian* commented, with approval, that the practice was 'more humoured [*sic*] in the breach than in the observance' and now 'almost unknown in the Colonies . . . . Our great New Year is kept in a manner more becoming Christians than it was in the days of our fathers.' First footing 'led to much evil, and recalled some of the worst features of the pagan festivals', whose great fault was that they were 'born in superstition'.[51] There are, however, reports of first footers throughout the country and the nineteenth century, and in some districts, such as rural Southland, the custom survived into the late twentieth century. In Wellington, at New Year of 1874, the 'ceremony of "first footing" was not allowed to lapse, and many a Scotchman's house was made lively by a sudden rush of visitors, who, after a short stay, were again off to some other chiel's place'.[52] Note, though, that only Scottish homes received a visit. In the small settlement of Kelso, in West Otago, 'Most of the people who had gone to bed had a visit from "first-footers" and roysterers' in the early hours of New Year 1882.[53] Perhaps, elsewhere, the practice simply became private and local. In the colonial situation many migrants lived alongside neighbours from very different backgrounds and no doubt those unfamiliar with first footing experienced some alarm if they found strangers knocking on their doors after midnight. It is likely that most first footers kept their visits to family and friends rather than the entire neighbourhood, which in their homeland would have been seen as fair game.

Certainly the generally light-hearted and sociable practice of first footing could occasionally take a rather more sinister turn. In Hampden, just north of Dunedin, a correspondent complained, late in the century, that on New Year's Eve 'a band of larrikins, half drunk, paraded the township, visiting the houses of the visitors (at least those who had no men in the house), battering at the doors, trying the windows, and demanding whisky'.[54] There was, noted an indignant reporter from Ngaruawahia in 1875, 'a distinction between knocking at a person's door and wishing him a happy New Year, and kicking at it so violently that his first outlay must be a coat of paint'. Almost everybody was 'prepared to take a joke on New Year's Eve', but things could go too far. 'There is a difference between being joked with by those with whom you are on good terms and by those you have never seen nor heard of in your life.'[55]

From the 1870s, the press almost invariably labelled noisy and reckless behaviour larrikinism, as when the *Otago Witness* commented at New Year 1879 that 'amongst the crowds, larrikins made themselves as prominent as it is the use and wont of larrikin nature to do'.[56] The term larrikin, which possibly originated from Melbourne, was a new colonial term for a 'street rowdy', often a juvenile.[57] Much of the larrikins' revelry was relatively harmless, and seen as such by the rest of the community, which expected a little misbehaviour at New Year. The 'usual "foolishments" were indulged in by the stay-awakes, who look upon New Year's morn as a time when they may run riot at pleasure', reported an Auckland paper in 1874.[58] Sometimes the revellers wore masks, like the 'frolicsome lads and young men, wearing hideous masks or false faces', who mingled with the crowd at Auckland's Queen Street wharf in 1881; or a 'number of elderly boys' who marked New Year of 1882 in Hamilton wearing 'false faces, and went on an expedition of semi-madness round the town, burlesquingly garrotting their friends, who however took the fun as best suited them'.[59]

Besides shouting and the inevitable firecrackers, popular activities for 'larrikins' included knocking on doors and running away, as in Auckland where 'a number of "young bloods"' hurried 'from door to door hammering with knockers or pulling at bells, to let sleepers know that the year of grace 1877 had begun'.[60] Marking buildings was another way to take note of the New Year. In New Plymouth, the midnight tolling of church bells was followed by 'that nonsensical practice of disfiguring the doors and premises of all the shops closed, by chalking on them "1890"'.[61] Elsewhere, the marks were more permanent. Ponsonby residents suffered an 'instance of wantonly destructive larrikinism' at New Year 1888, when a 'number of miscreants . . . daubed and smeared almost everything within their reach with a plentiful supply of coal tar. The church, windows and walls, garden fences, shop shutters, an express cart, and even a live horse were the objects upon which these hoodlums expended their mischievous energies'.[62]

Other popular activities for the rowdiest New Year's Eve revellers included turning over sheds and out-buildings, moving carts and, most common of all, 'the sacred rite of gate-lifting' – removing gates from their hinges.[63] Occasionally larrikins caused more serious destruction, as at Wanganui in 1879, when they broke the windows of a bank, post office and newspaper office, among other buildings.[64] Of course, damaging gates could also have serious consequences at a time when many people kept livestock and grew their own fruit and vegetables. In the small Otago town of Waitahuna, as a New Year's Eve precaution many householders 'padlocked all their portable property' and 'patrolled their premises until 3 o'clock, or thereabouts . . . keeping a vigilant eye (not always with success) on the mischievous youths who were about in no small numbers'. Despite these efforts, in a couple of cases 'serious mischief was done by the removal of gates, thereby letting cattle into gardens'.[65]

Some residents succeeded in frightening larrikins away with more active methods than patrolling their property. In 1884, for example, a Tapanui carrier saw 'some sportive youths . . . dragging a Chinaman's cart down the road'. He 'fired at them with blank cartridge, causing a general stampede'.[66] The following decade, in nearby Waikoikoi, a woman fed up with the practical jokes being played on her household determined 'to put a stop to it if possible. Thinking that they would be up to their old games on New Year's Eve she perched up in the branches of a gum tree in the garden and awaited events.' When, at two in the morning, two men started removing the buggy from the back yard 'she descended from her perch and made after them'. One offender ran away, the other got caught in the barbed-wire fence: 'The brave woman rushed at him and belaboured him soundly with a stick. She thinks it will be a lesson to the other larrikins.'[67]

Newspapers reported the triumph of respectable householders over larrikins with glee. Rowdy midnight revelry came under increasing fire from critics as the century progressed, and the general community developed an increasing intolerance towards riotous New Year behaviour. This shift reflected changing middle-class visions of respectability. By the late nineteenth century, moral crusaders became increasingly concerned about wild colonial children, promoted the cult of domesticity and, above all, battled the 'demon' drink.[68] The economic depression experienced in some parts of the country during the 1880s and 1890s may also have accelerated middle-class fears of social unrest. The drunken public revelry once accepted as a natural part of the New Year festivities now encountered staunch criticism.

·ﻦ

In some parts of New Zealand and particularly in the earlier years of European settlement, New Year's Eve had never been a rowdy occasion. It is noticeable that the level of Scottish migration in a district corresponded closely with the level of New Year's Eve revelry. Taranaki – the nineteenth-century province with the lowest proportion of Scots in the population – certainly experienced quieter New Years than did the most Scottish provinces – Southland and Otago – where even small rural settlements celebrated the coming in of the new year with vigour. Christchurch was another place where New Year's Eve excited little public display. While districts with more Scottish migrants celebrated the season with whisky drinking, first footing, fireworks and bands, in districts where English colonists were most dominant the most visible sign of the coming of another year was of an entirely different nature – attendance at special 'watch night' church services.

The Protestant watch night service was a particularly English tradition, developed by early Methodists in the eighteenth century, although it had a counterpart in the older Catholic practice of keeping vigil – staying awake and holding devotions – on the night before a festival. Initially these Methodist watch nights took place on a variety of occasions, but they eventually became centred on the New Year.[69] New Year watch night services became increasingly prevalent in nineteenth-century England, spreading to Baptist, Congregational and Anglican churches (although some Anglican clergy disapproved of the service because, although popular, it fell outside the traditional liturgical calendar). By the late nineteenth century the watch night performed an important part in the popular piety of the English urban working classes. Although many were not regular Sunday churchgoers, they took part in the rites of Christian baptism and marriage, and came in large numbers to the hugely popular harvest festivals and New Year watch nights. This popularity had much to do with concepts of 'luck': many believed that seeing in the New Year at church would ensure God's blessing for the coming year.[70]

English migrants brought the watch night with them to New Zealand where, in mixed communities, it provided a vivid contrast with Scottish New Year's Eve traditions. The 'good city of Wellington' ushered in 1869 with a great mixture of events: 'sacred chantings, solemn Te Deums, religious services, the strains of martial music, singing and dancing, a display of sky rockets, the firing of cannon, the huzzas of the people in the streets re-echoed by our seamen in harbour'.[71] In 1875 an Oamaru reporter noted that the watch night service of the local Wesleyans 'presented a wonderful contrast to the saturnalia and larrikins' jubilee which prevailed in the streets at the time'.[72] Certainly such services had a serious tone. The typical Methodist watch night began at about 11 p.m. and included the hymns, prayers and sermons of a regular service, though selected for their suitability to the occasion. As midnight approached, the churchgoers spent time in individual contemplation and prayer. 'The concluding portion of this service is very impressive', a Christchurch newspaper noted of the watch night at Durham Street Wesleyan Church in 1873. 'Just before midnight the whole congregation kneel and engage in silent prayer. When midnight is passed and the New Year fully commenced, they rise and join in singing the hymn "Come let us anew our journey pursue." The Benediction is then pronounced, and the congregation, after wishing each other a "Happy New Year," depart to their homes.'[73]

Sermons at these watch nights generally reviewed the struggles and blessings of the year about to pass, and urged a renewed Christian commitment for the year to come. Typically, at New Plymouth's Wesleyan Church on 31 December 1884, one preacher, Mr Lee, 'exhorted his congregation to strive to put the future to a better use than had

Methodists outside the Maori Church at Taumutu, near Lake Ellesmere, Canterbury, in the late nineteenth century. Methodists generally saw in the New Year at watch night church services. WILLIAM MORLEY, *HISTORY OF METHODISM IN NEW ZEALAND*, MCKEE, WELLINGTON, 1900, P. 187.

been done with the past'. A second preacher, Mr Collis, 'passed in review the blessings of the dying year'.[74] On the first Sunday of the year, Methodists had another opportunity to renew their spiritual commitment at the covenant service, when 'they are invited to enter into or renew their covenant with Almighty God, that by His aid and in dependence upon Divine Grace, they will, in the year upon which they have entered, and during their whole lives, devote themselves fully to Him'.[75] New Year was, clearly, a significant spiritual occasion for more devout Methodists, such as Thomas Ferens, a young teacher at the Wesleyan mission at Waikouaiti, north of Dunedin. On 31 December 1848 he 'awoke with many sad reflective thoughts of past, present, and future things'. Together with a servant and missionaries Charles and Eliza Creed, Ferens 'Watched the close of the old year, and the New Year in by prayer . . . Thank God for so many mercies, and of Health and of many friends'. Later, as a North Otago runholder, he held watch night services at his station for family and staff. For Ferens New Year was a 'solemn time – serious remembrance of the past – and a solemn view of the future!'[76]

Methodists may have been the most enthusiastic proponents of the watch night service, but they were by no means the only New Zealand congregations to observe the practice. At New Year 1880, residents of Nelson had a choice of watch night services at the Anglican Cathedral, St John's Wesleyan Church, or the Baptist and Congregational Churches.[77] Like the Methodist watch nights, the services in other churches conformed fairly closely to a regular evening service, with prayers and addresses selected to suit the occasion. At St Paul's Anglican Cathedral, Auckland, in 1880, Reverend Charles Nelson read a portion of the evening service, delivered a special sermon, and then 'a very large number remained' to partake of the first holy communion of the year.[78] Anglican New Year sermons, like Methodist ones, encouraged hearers to review, in a spiritual sense, the year that had passed and resolve to do better in the year about to begin. In 1878 Reverend Nelson urged his watch night congregation at the cathedral 'to devote more time in the future than they had in the past, to their preparation for another and unending world, and exhorted them to stand by and adhere to the good resolutions which they should make for better conduct of their lives'.[79]

These services were clearly serious rather than celebratory occasions, with the dark night-time atmosphere adding to the solemnity, although in some churches decorations of greenery, possibly lingering from Christmas, cheered the churchgoers. Occasionally churches had special decorations just for New Year. In 1874 All Saints' Anglican Church, Dunedin, was 'very prettily decorated with moss' – symbolic, perhaps, of decay and the passing of time.[80] The diary of Mary Taylor (daughter of the notable Wanganui missionary Richard Taylor) reveals the impact a watch night could have upon a devout Anglican. 'How solemn was the service & yet how joyful', she wrote after attending the service on New Year's Eve 1858, recalling 'the cordial shake with all, native alike so hearty & genuine, oh may it indeed be a happy year & blessed to all of us – how will it find us next? How many of those solemn vows, made in the night season will be remembered how many kept.'[81] Anglican and Methodist Maori (the majority of Maori converts to Christianity), particularly the Methodists, adopted the watch night along with other traditions of these churches.

Among the colonists, though, the watch night remained a distinctly English tradition. Presbyterian New Year's Eve services were extremely rare, unless the day happened to be a Sunday or the night of a regular weekly prayer meeting, when reference might be made to the occasion during the usual evening service. When Presbyterians in Hamilton held a watch night in 1886 it had a distinctly non-English feel to it – after the service the congregation gathered for refreshments and 'an hour was spent in social intercourse', a reflection of the sociable rather than spiritual nature of most Scottish New Year's Eve celebrations.[82]

But if Presbyterians seldom held watch nights, the more pious among them did not treat New Year as a purely social occasion. Like the more spiritually aware of other denominations, for some Presbyterians this was a time to reflect seriously upon their faith. 'The New Year is a time of mirth and perhaps it should be so, but we should join trembling with our mirth', wrote conservative Waikouaiti minister John Christie. 'We stand on the brink of eternity. It is a time for serious thought . . . How brief is life! We do not know that another year shall be granted us to live . . . . Let us devote ourselves anew to [God], and consecrate our lives to his glory.'[83] Numerous Presbyterian diaries reveal that the devout made New Year a season for reviewing their spiritual as well as material progress. As 1863 drew to a close, Taieri farm labourer William Muir recalled that 'I was exactly at the line [crossing the Equator] when I com[m]enced this year and now in the providence of God I have nearly seen its close. Now I may say that the Lord has conducted me through many seen and many more unseen dangers . . . . Thou hast been my help. Leave me not nor forsake me.'[84]

The New Year thoughts of Otago Peninsula farmer and builder Walter Riddell, also a faithful Presbyterian, reveal a more explicit concern with material progress. Although he would later achieve financial success, in the 1860s Riddell struggled to support his family. At New Year 1866 he recorded: 'I am entering another year with £83 debt on my head, with plenty of hard work before me and if God grant me my health I will be a clear man in another year. I have increased in the year that has passed, a house, an acre of land cleared 15 hens, 2 cows and a son.'[85] Although Riddell concentrated more than most diarists on his material wealth, he did not lack concern for spiritual matters. His material gains he saw as a blessing from God, as his prayer for New Year 1869 makes clear: 'Lord create in me a thankful heart & a loving heart unto Thee for all thy goodness and mercy towards me and mine and keep thy hand around us through the year we have begun. Grant thy spirit to abide with us. Teach us thy way O Lord.'[86] In his study of the wealthy in Otago and Canterbury, many of whom came from humble backgrounds, Jim McAloon notes the existence of 'a powerful ideology, that equated advancement with individual merit'.[87] This ideology had its roots in Protestant concepts of providence, whereby God blessed the spiritually worthy. For a man like Walter Riddell, the material and the spiritual were powerfully linked.

Just like individuals, communities also reviewed their progress at New Year. This is seen most obviously in newspaper editorials, which almost invariably took the opportunity to assess the progress of their district and of the country. 'The advent of a new year', began the *Otago Witness*'s 1857 New Year editorial, 'is a marked time in human life, and a period in the history of a young and rising colony, which call for grave reflections, and afford a point from which we are enabled to reflect upon past events, and to speculate upon our future prospects'.[88] Likewise, a New Year 1865 editorial from Auckland's *New Zealand Herald* noted that a 'wise Merchant . . . naturally at this season takes stock, and reviews the business of the year. He thus gets accurate information of a most valuable character to guide his operations for the future. The same conduct ought to be pursued by communities, municipal and national'.[89] The press thus reflected an important facet of nineteenth-century New Zealand's New Year: for Presbyterian diarists, Methodist and Anglican watch nighters and English newspaper editors alike, this was the season for stocktaking.

American historian of holidays Leigh Schmidt argues that the 'more-secular' New Year's resolutions for self-improvement, so widespread today, first became popular at the turn of the twentieth century, born of the older Christian practice of 'pious resolution'.[90] Certainly I have found no evidence in nineteenth-century New Zealand of these 'secular' resolutions, while there are plenty of 'pious' ones. As 1859 drew to a close, the meditations of Mary Taylor of Wanganui led her to long for 'the happy world where is not sorrow or sin – oh help me to prepare for it & give me a more thankful heart – & good resolves for the New Year, that it may be more happy than the last – to live in the world but not of it'.[91] Donald McLean, the government agent and politician notorious for his role in the purchase of Maori land for European settlement, spent New Year's Day 1849 at a large hui at Rewarewa, on the Kapiti coast, discussing land issues. This was, he noted, a contrast to the 'day of great enjoyment and festivity in Scotland'. But this Highland gentleman also spared time to assess his spiritual state – 'I fear this year finds me little in advance of last year' – and to pray 'that if spared for another year I shall be found a better and wiser and more sincere Christian'.[92]

New Zealanders' varying ethnic backgrounds and religious persuasions determined the way they celebrated New Year's Eve in the nineteenth century. For New Year's Day, however, there was widespread agreement – on this, the colony's most widely observed holiday, everyone hoped to indulge in a little outdoor recreation.

Scottish migrants often followed the custom of their homeland, gathering with family and friends to enjoy the holiday, sometimes travelling quite a distance to do so. Robert Nicol, an Oamaru flour miller, travelled to Balclutha for a reunion with his siblings: 'the Nicol family met on New Years day and we spent a very pleasant and profitable time'.[93] Even domestic servants regularly received a holiday on New Year's Day, a reflection of the importance of the occasion. This allowed them to visit friends and relations or attend some of the local attractions, even while it curtailed somewhat the activities of more elite households. As a Dunedin society columnist noted in 1896: 'As usual on [New Year's Day], there were some family gatherings and small picnics were also indulged in; but as it is a day which is generally given to the servants of the house for their holiday, most people entertain as little as possible at that time'.[94]

Families of more modest means did not hesitate to gather in large numbers. Many combined a family gathering with an excursion or picnic, sometimes followed by a dance. In 1861, Dunedin merchant George Hepburn

> spent a very happy New Years day, all our family being together, the young folks with some acquaintances forming a party of 13 set all off for a ride to the Taieri Plain. I accompanied

them for 12 miles, where Geo & I called upon an old friend & had lunch & returned – the party went on to the river about 5 miles further after resting & enjoying themselves a while they all returned in safety to Tea. Then had a dance in the barn & parted good friends.[95]

Wellingtonians were out in force on New Year's Day 1861, taking the opportunity to explore the district by whatever means were at hand. As usual, many visited the Hutt Valley, then an

interesting rural district . . . . We noticed a great number of Picnic parties, distributed in different parts of the valley, and all seemed joyous and happy. There were also numerous visitors to Porirua Bay, and several picnic parties at Ohariu. Sailing excursions also had their attractions with many. The June, Emerald Isle, Pearl, and other small craft, were engaged conveying holiday folk to Soame's Island, Lowry Bay, and round the harbour; and every one seemed determined to make it a real day of pleasure.[96]

Often, the trip to a holiday resort formed a large part of the holiday entertainment. Unlike today, when public transport is limited on holidays, nineteenth-century transport operators increased their services and kept remarkably busy catering for excursionists. On the 1899 New Year holiday in Christchurch, for example, 13,500 people travelled by train to Lyttelton, and 'a large number' took 'the morning trains to Rangiora, Dunsandel and Methven . . . while the two express trains for the south were heavily laden with excursionists'. Meanwhile, the 'Christchurch Tramway Company carried 14,000 passengers over its lines during the day, 5000 being taken to Sumner, and 2500 to the Show Grounds'.[97]

The crowded state of public transport could make for an exciting journey, like that described by 14-year-old Edward Roberts of Dunedin in his diary for New Year's Day 1898. He and his friends caught a train up the coast for a picnic at Waitati, then a two-hour trip. When they arrived at the Dunedin railway station to begin their journey, there was such a crowd of would-be travellers that they could not get on the train. Determined to carry all the excursionists, the railway department made special arrangements:

At last they shunted on some open trucks with tarpaulins over them into one of which we managed to scramble . . . . Going through the Deborah Bay tunnel we had a lovely

The transport to a picnic provided much of the day's entertainment. These turn-of-the-century Blenheim picnickers (probably a Methodist church group) could choose to travel by bicycle or in carts towed by a traction engine. PHOTOGRAPH FROM THE COLLECTION OF ROBERT AND ANNA BREWER, F-66516-1/2, ALEXANDER TURNBULL LIBRARY, WELLINGTON.

experience. It is a very long tunnel and we were going extra slowly. Being in an open truck we were nearly suffocated by smoke and our clothes were saturated with steam. It was a horrible experience.

After disembarking they had an hour's walk 'along a road beautifully wooded on either side' to their picnic place, where they spent an enjoyable day eating, playing and catching crayfish in the creek. They caught the 9 p.m. express train home, and this time 'most of us scrambled onto a first class carriage and we had only 2nd class tickets. This was to make up for coming out in the truck. I was out on the "birdcage" all the way home and it was grand.' In honour of the holiday the train's engine had a special message painted on its headlight – 'A good new year to all'.[98]

New Year outings and gatherings frequently expanded beyond families, sometimes involving the entire community. This was especially the case in rural districts, such as Carterton, which in 1862 was 'a village hewn out of the wilderness within the last four years'. On New Year's Day about 50 adults and 60 children gathered at the Fairbrothers' property for 'a sumptuous repast, the produce of the district'. Later they sang and danced until dawn.[99] Likewise, for the small West Otago farming community of Kelso, 1 January 1883 'was a red-letter day in this district. Mr and Mrs McKellar, of Brooksdale, invited the whole country to a picnic, and I should say that at least 750 responded to their kind invitation by presenting themselves at Brooksdale'. The local newspaper correspondent had 'never been at a more enjoyable gathering, and all I came in contact with were equally delighted'.[100]

Among the largest of nineteenth-century picnics were those arranged by community organisations, such as the friendly societies. Friendly societies, which provided sick and funeral benefits to members, played an important financial role in the days before government provided welfare. Just as appealing, though, were the convivial aspects of belonging to one of these organisations, which gloried in some magnificent names – the most important were the Ancient Order of Foresters, the Ancient Order of Druids, and the Manchester Unity Independent Order of Oddfellows. Besides their regular meetings, the friendly societies enjoyed nothing as much as a parade or a picnic, at which they were generally joined by family and friends.[101] Most held their anniversary, for convenience, on a public holiday. Queen's Birthday (24 May) and the Prince of Wales's Birthday (11 November) were popular, while others preferred to celebrate at Easter or New Year. To give just one example, one of the largest New Year events in the

Picnics could be huge community affairs, as the parking area for this 'monster picnic' at Greytown, c.1900, indicates. PHOTOGRAPH BY FRANK MAY REYNOLDS, F-55983-1/2, R. E. CAMPBELL COLLECTION, ALEXANDER TURNBULL LIBRARY, WELLINGTON.

Wellington district during the 1850s was the annual picnic, preceded by a procession, of the Rose of the Valley Lodge of Odd Fellows, based in the Hutt Valley.[102] Temperance organisations were also great holders of picnics. On New Year's Day 1857, while the Rose of the Valley supporters no doubt enjoyed a beverage or three at their picnic, the Port Nicholson Total Abstinence Society attracted 300 people to their 'temperance soiree and social gathering' at Mr Wilkinson's tea gardens in Oriental Bay.[103]

Probably the most widespread and popular of New Zealand's nineteenth-century picnics were those arranged by Sunday schools, most often held at Christmas or New Year. Sunday schools were hugely influential institutions in colonial New Zealand. In Otago and Southland in the 1860s just over half of all school-age children were enrolled in Sunday school, with 75 per cent attending in an average week. By the end of the century, three-quarters of the province's children appeared on the rolls, the increase occurring after education became officially 'secular' with the passing of the 1877 Education Act.[104] The annual picnic formed a highlight of the Sunday-school year, and attracted great crowds – it 'is looked forward to by the children for a long time', Frederick Haslam wrote to his mother, describing the Albert Street Congregational Church's Sunday-school picnic. A thousand children, plus their parents and teachers, attended the 1864 New Year's Day picnic, combined with that of another Auckland Congregationalist Sunday school. It took place in the popular Auckland Domain, where other holidaymakers also strolled the grounds and listened to the performance of the band of the 50th Regiment, which played there every Saturday afternoon. 'Altogether it formed a grand concourse of enjoyment', declared Haslam. 'We had 60 or 70 swings, a boat swing, all kinds of games, and in such a beautiful place to play in, the Domain is now most beautiful, and its lovely walks . . . . There might be perhaps 4000 people altogether in the walks and up at the swings. It looked like fairyland. I never had anything like it in England.'[105]

Sunday schools often combined together for their picnics. At Christchurch, on New Year's Day 1869, about 1500 children from twelve different Sunday schools (five Wesleyan, two Free Methodist, two Presbyterian and three Baptist) attended the annual Sunday School Union treat. After mustering in Cathedral Square they sang a couple of hymns, then marched in procession, bearing the banners of their various schools, to the site of their picnic, a paddock in Armagh Street. There they enjoyed a variety of games, not to mention lunch and tea. 'It would have cheered the heart, even of a disciple of the late Mr Malthus, to witness the hearty glee of the children', reported the local newspaper.[106] By the 1880s the Sunday School Union, which provided support and resources for various Protestant denominations, was a force to be reckoned with. In Auckland, its annual New Year picnic at the Domain attracted several thousand children, along with hundreds of teachers. In 1887 they provided a new treat for onlookers – accompanied by the Garrison Band, over 3000 children joined together to sing several hymns and the national anthem.[107] In other districts, separate Sunday schools held

Children of Port Chalmers Presbyterian Sunday school gathered for their annual picnic in December 1893. PHOTOGRAPH BY DAVID DE MAUS, P-L2I-5, PRESBYTERIAN CHURCH ARCHIVES, DUNEDIN.

separate picnics. On New Year's Day 1895 at Hokitika, the Anglican Sunday school held a picnic in Cass Square, the Presbyterian Sunday school at Glossop's, and the Wesleyan Sunday school at Cassidy's paddock. 'The children have something of a grievance in being restricted to one picnic instead of having the run of three, as would have been the case were the picnics held on different days', reported the newspaper.[108] Clearly attendance at many of these picnics was not restricted to regular students of the Sunday school concerned, but to all interested children in the community.

Picnics were, undoubtedly, one of the great institutions of nineteenth-century life. Whether large or small, and whomever arranged by – Sunday school, club, community or family and friends – picnics provided a welcome diversion from the hard-working

Picnics could be fairly small gatherings of family and friends, like this group near New Plymouth. Surveyor and ethnologist Percy Smith is on the far right of the group. F-28204-1/2, CROMPTON-SMITH COLLECTION, ALEXANDER TURNBULL LIBRARY, WELLINGTON.

grind of everyday life. The clothes worn by nineteenth-century picnickers made for striking photographs. Rather than dressing casually, colonial picnickers wore their Sunday best in recognition of the special occasion. They could also take considerable trouble over the food. Alexander Don, who spent many years in Central Otago as a missionary to the Chinese, attended the Arrowtown Sunday-school picnics held 'under the beautiful weeping willows' beside Lake Hayes on New Year's Day. For these events, the refreshments were 'collected by means of a dray; at any rate, the catering was on a liberal and lavish scale, on the lines of an open-air banquet, the tables being laden with hams, poultry, joints, and cookies of all descriptions'.[109] Any large picnic involving children invariably offered cakes, buns and lollies as treats.

This charming group of mothers and children, photographed by James McAllister of Stratford around 1900. Note that everyone is dressed in their finest clothes. G-7894-I/I, JAMES MCALLISTER COLLECTION, ALEXANDER TURNBULL LIBRARY, WELLINGTON.

This picnic gathering at Bon Accord, the large property of James Adam near Milton, features bowls (on the left) and other games. It was common for large picnics to include organised games and activities.
C/NEG SHEET 156/5/E, HOCKEN COLLECTIONS, UARE TAOKA O HAKENA, UNIVERSITY OF OTAGO.

The chance to socialise with friends and neighbours, take a trip to an interesting location and be treated to special food formed a large part of the appeal of a picnic, but most nineteenth-century outings also offered additional attractions in the form of outdoor games. At smaller picnics, these were generally fairly spontaneous or informal. A good example is the annual New Year's Day picnic held at Dublin Bay by the settlers of Fork Run, east of Lake Wanaka. In 1897 about 30 attended, and after a 'substantial repast' the older people 'sat under the shade of the manuka trees discussing the leading topics of the day'. Meanwhile, the youngsters played games, revealing diverse cultural influences by choosing to play both shinty, a hockey-like sport from the Scottish Highlands, and the American favourite, baseball. The picnickers gathered again that evening at William Kingan's house for a dance.[110] Party and chasing games proved popular picnic pastimes for children, as at Dunedin's Wesleyan Sunday-school New

A women's foot race at the Harihari sports, Westland. Rural sports often included events for men and women, boys and girls, and a wide range of novelty events. CP 2500, 477-K&L, PETER LUCAS COLLECTION, MACMILLAN BROWN LIBRARY, UNIVERSITY OF CANTERBURY.

Year picnic in 1871, where 'kiss-in-the-ring and scrambling for lollies were conspicuous' among the games enjoyed.[111]

Larger picnics called for more-organised activities, and frequently included athletic competitions. Everybody present had the opportunity to participate, as events catered to all ages and interests. Separate foot races might be held, for example, for men and women, boys and girls. Baby contests ensured that even the youngest members of the community had the opportunity to win a prize. Many of the events were more for fun than for serious competition. At the 'monster picnic' held in Chisholm's Bush, South Auckland, at New Year 1870 for the pupils of Papakura, Drury and Wairoa Road Schools, Janet Brisbane won the girls' contests for hopping and jumping, while Milly Worthington was judged 'the girl who could laugh the heartiest'. Harriet Harding earned an 'artificial wreath of red and green for the prettiest school-girl on the ground' and, just to prove good looks were not essential to success, a similar wreath went to 'the plainest school-girl'. 'Miss Anderson, on her own confession', earned this dubious honour.[112] Prizes, donated by local well-wishers or obtained through fundraising by the organisers, included both cash and goods. At the 'annual village gathering' at Papanui, Christchurch, in 1889, a wide variety of events took place. The men's and boys' contests all led to cash prizes, but evidently the organisers thought that women would prefer to receive useful household goods, such as the bag of sugar, leg of ham and bag of oatmeal won by Mrs Prentice, Mrs Kemp and Mrs Beal respectively in one of the married women's foot races.[113]

・➤

Sports were the reason for many nineteenth-century New Year gatherings. New Zealand colonists used the term 'sports' to refer to a local gathering, invariably on a holiday, for a series of competitive events. As at picnics, the games varied from serious athletic contests to novelty events, and many also included cultural events such as competitions in dancing or musical performance. A typical example is the Rangiora sports, held on New Year's Day 1889, attracting a crowd of about 1800 to the Domain. The contests included foot and bicycle races (one solely for Maori), a bicycle obstacle race, a walking match, high jump, pole vault, hurdle race, sack race, dancing (sailors' hornpipe, Highland fling and Irish jig), wrestling matches, a fire brigade competition and a baby show.[114]

The organisation of sports was occasionally informal, with just a few locals getting together to raise prize money and plan the events. More commonly, though, a national or friendly society or an individual (typically a hotel-keeper or large employer) sponsored and ran the sports. If no other suitable ground were available, events took place in the street, as with the Christmas sports of the Arrowtown goldminers, recalled by David Mackie:

> They'd have the street all decorated up. And they'd have the horses and the men, all the sports was in the main street. They used to gallop up and down there . . . there'd be high jump, hop step and jump, wrasslin', and what do you call that . . . tilting in the ring. Oh there was all sorts of sports. Quoits. Tossing the caber.[115]

George Te Koeti competes in the pole vault at the Okarito sports, Westland, in the early twentieth century. Maori frequently participated in field sports, athletics, horse racing and boating events during the nineteenth century, often with great success. At some gatherings there were special events for Maori, while at others they competed alongside Pakeha. PHOTOGRAPH BY G. R. NORTHCROFT, CP 2787, 128-32&33, A. C. GRAHAM COLLECTION, MACMILLAN BROWN LIBRARY, UNIVERSITY OF CANTERBURY.

Maori enjoyed these athletic contests, and in some districts organised sports for the whole community. At Kohanga, in the Waikato, New Year's Day 1873 featured 'sports of various kinds got up by the Europeans and Maoris' and attended by numerous Maori and Pakeha from the surrounding districts. A local mill owner donated 'a fat ox, which was cooked in Maori style, as was also a large heap of potatoes'. The day ended with Maori and Rarotongan dancing, the latter accompanied by music 'obtained from a tin dish'. A 'greater amount of fun could not be had in any other district', reported the local newspaper correspondent.[116]

No discussion of colonial sports days could be complete without a mention of horse racing. In an era when horses were one of the most important means of transport and also provided the power for farming and other industries, racing was an accessible and hugely popular sport. Horse racing frequently took place, for convenience, on holidays, and every tiny settlement had its regular meeting. Many races started as fairly casual affairs, with the nearest beach providing a convenient course – in the 1860s, the residents of Russell enjoyed New Year's Day races at 'the long sandy beach of Oneroa', while some Wellingtonians travelled north to Pauatahanui to follow the races on the beach there.[117] Publicans often contributed greatly to the day's events, as at the 'capital day's racing' enjoyed by 1500 or so miners at Stoney Creek Flat, near Queenstown, at New Year 1864. Mr Bracken of the Camp Hotel, Maori Point, ran the grandstand, 'a handsome erection, comfortably fitted up and provided with private rooms', and two other publicans ran 'booths of more humble pretensions'. The miners evidently appreciated the refreshments provided, with one of the booths taking over £70 of their hard-won cash. It was a day of 'the greatest harmony and good feeling'. The five races ranged from the three-mile Miners' Purse, worth 30 sovereigns and won by Fly-a-way, to a hack race, in which Black Bess won the 10-sovereign prize from a field of nine.[118]

By the late nineteenth century horse racing had become a much more sophisticated affair, in the larger towns at least, with racing clubs, jockey clubs and impressive grounds and grandstands. One of the largest New Year meetings was at Ellerslie, where the Auckland Cup racing attracted a crowd of over 10,000 in 1899. Auckland Cup Day was 'fast becoming the most important racing event in the colony', declared the *Auckland Weekly News*, even if Canterbury did claim 'the honour of the New Zealand Cup'.[119] In Canterbury, the main event of New Year's day was the annual Lyttelton regatta. Crowds gathered at the port to watch the sailing and rowing races, with swimming races added to the attractions during the 1890s. Those who had little interest in water sports could enjoy the 'land sports' in one of the main streets, with the usual mixture of athletic and novelty contests.[120]

Although the Sunday-school annual treats, monster picnics, local sports gatherings and horse races were popular at New Year, another occasion outshone them all:

A large crowd (estimated at over 10,000) gathered at the Ellerslie racecourse, Auckland, for 'Cup Day', New Year 1899. Here race-goers stroll on the lawn. AUCKLAND WEEKLY NEWS, 6 JANUARY 1899, SUPPLEMENT, P. 1. 7-A293, SPECIAL COLLECTIONS, AUCKLAND CITY LIBRARIES.

the Caledonian games. Caledonian games proved a highlight of the holiday in many a colonial community, flourishing wherever a few Scottish migrants could be mustered. Often, as with sports and horse races, the early events were fairly informal and spontaneous affairs. On the Dunstan goldfields, at New Year 1864, a 'sort of impromptu local Caledonian Society' was formed on 31 December and ran 'a very decent gathering, and some right good sports' the following day. Along with the running, jumping, wrestling and novelty races which might be seen at any colonial sports day, this gathering included the strength events that typified Caledonian games – throwing the heavy stone or light stone and tossing the caber. Although no pipers – another important feature of most Caledonian gatherings – are mentioned in the newspaper report, a 'little lad named Munro danced the Highland fling capitally amidst tremendous applause'. After accounting for expenses and prizes, this swiftly organised event made an impressive profit of £19, donated to the local hospital.[121]

Publicans often had a hand in organising early Caledonian games, as they did other sports events. In Dunedin, the first Caledonian games, held on New Year's Day 1862, were the responsibility of Shadrach Jones, an English doctor whose skills as an entrepreneur led him to run two very successful hotels, the Vauxhall Gardens and two theatres.[122] He had already held 'Old English sports' a week earlier on Boxing Day. The labels 'Old English' and 'Caledonian' were perhaps devices to increase patronage by their appeal to nostalgia and national pride, for the two events differed little, except that the Caledonian sports featured 'a Gaelic inscription, which, we are informed, meant "Happiness to all," . . . displayed above the entrance'. (Both events included Scottish dancing.)[123] James Strachan, a young goldminer who came to Dunedin over Christmas and New Year to take a break and spend some of his earnings from the Tuapeka field, was impressed with Jones's business abilities. Amongst all the entertainments on offer, the Caledonian games appealed most to this Fifeshire native:

> Then to get up Caledonian Sports at the shortest notice [Jones] cut off one side of the stable [of the Provincial Hotel] and turned it into a Sports ring. He could not manage 100 yds but he had it run in two 50's there and back. We had a man in kilts who ran second in the 100 with them on, and one the high jump in his trunks. Then we had the Hammers and Stone, Long Jump, and what I have very seldom seen out here – Hitch and Kick [a form of long jump]. Altogether we had a great day's sport.[124]

Allan Maclean, the runholder at Ardgour, near Tarras in Central Otago, organised games as a treat for his workers. In 1873, concerned that his shepherds might not return if tempted away from the run for Christmas and New Year recreation, he provided Caledonian games at home. Free beer for all hands and the presence of three Highland pipers ensured a lively and successful day's entertainment.[125] In other districts, Caledonian games began as community picnics, but as the population grew and transport improved more formal events evolved. An example is the event known by the 1880s as the Warepa and Kaihiku Caledonian Gathering. This began as an annual community picnic held in a natural clearing in the bush at Warepa, South Otago. As John Wilson described it,

> all and sundry laid out their viands on snowy white cloths. Every one contributed to the general provision, and the biggest pots that could be requisitioned in the district were slung on poles to boil the water for the tea. At first the sports were started for the children and juniors, but soon events for adults were added . . . . The fiddles were kept going, and dancing was kept up steadily on the green turf. Everyone knew everyone, and there was a homely, hearty feeling. When the picnics attracted strangers from all quarters, and it is said on several occasions several hundreds were present, they gradually developed into proper sports meetings.[126]

James Marchbanks recalled these same games from his boyhood summers, spent with friends farming at Kaihiku. The great occasion of the summer was New Year, when 'there was a lot of picnicking and Highland games, with pipers, dancing, putting the stone, tossing the caber, wrestling and running. This was kept up till evening, when they gathered at one another's farms, singing Scottish songs, danced and enjoyed themselves perhaps much more thoroughly than the young people do now.'[127]

Places both large and small took great pride in their Caledonian games. In Otago alone at least 23 towns and districts held these events in the nineteenth century. From Oamaru to Hyde, from Clyde to Kelso, crowds gathered to watch the sports and cultural events on offer. At Palmerston, with a borough population of just 800 people, the 1882 Caledonian games attracted 1200.[128] At their peak, in 1881, Dunedin's Caledonian games attracted 14,000 spectators on the first day of the two-day competition and invariably, from 1863 to 1900, the attendance ran to the thousands. As the *Otago Witness* commented in 1867, 'in the whole course of the year, there is

Punch depicts 'Mr New Chum' competing without success in a variety of events at Dunedin's Caledonian games – the foot race, sword dance, sword fight, sack race, climbing a greasy pole and tilting at the ring. OTAGO PUNCH, 5 JANUARY 1867, P. 148.

no popular assemblage which is more numerously or more readily attended than the [Caledonian] Society's gatherings'.[129] Most of these games took place on New Year's Day, but in South Otago something of a circuit developed, where competitors and spectators could attend the Owaka or Kaitangata games on Christmas Day, the Clutha games on Boxing Day, and the Clinton or Port Molyneux games on New Year's Day.[130] In Southland – by proportion of population the most Scottish of New Zealand's regions – Caledonian games were also particularly widespread and popular. At Invercargill, which then had a population of about 2500, the 'keenly contested' 1876 Caledonian games attracted some 4000 people. The games were of 'the well-known popular character, and comprised pibrochs on the Scottish bagpipes, quoits, throwing the light and heavy hammer, walking races, reel dancing, vaulting with the pole, wrestling, foot racing, and tilting at the ring'.[131]

But Caledonian games were not confined to the most Scottish areas of the colony – Caledonian societies, which generally ran most of these events in a more formal style by the end of the century, formed throughout the land. In Wellington, Scottish colonists held Highland sports on Christmas Day 1848, with shinty, hammer-throwing, wrestling and bagpipes.[132] In subsequent years, the Highlanders enjoyed shinty games at New Year, but Wellington's first large New Year Caledonian gathering – a great success with 'representatives of all classes' present – came in 1866.[133] In Auckland, a Caledonian gathering at New Year 1868 proved so successful that 'the kilted lads' held another gathering in 1869 at Mr Whitson's paddock, Newmarket, reported by the *Herald* as 'one of the greatest successes that could be imagined'.[134] Christchurch was slower to adopt the Caledonian New Year habit. In 1882 about 5000 people attended the 'first Caledonian gathering ever attempted in Christchurch . . . . It was a most successful athletic meeting . . . . In those items of the programme more peculiarly Scotch great interest was manifested, and it must have done many a Scotchman's patriotic heart good to hear Murdo Elder's strathspeys and reels, and see McRae's skilful "lifting" in the Ghillie Callum.'[135]

Some districts preferred the term 'Highland games' for events which were essentially identical to the Caledonian games of other localities. Two examples, which flourish to this day, are the Turakina Highland Games (first held in 1864) and the Waipu Highland Games (which commenced in 1871).[136] Both took place in communities founded by Highland Scots. Elsewhere, though, the Caledonian label proved more fitting, for the great majority of Scottish migrants to New Zealand (over 90 per cent) came from the Lowlands.[137] Caledonia – the Roman name for Scotland – was a term of great pride, a reminder that the Scots had remained invincible against the might of the Roman Empire. Although it referred, in a strict historical sense, only to the Highlands, by the nineteenth century this common poetic name was widely used to describe Scotland as a whole.[138] All New Zealand Scots could identify themselves as Caledonian, so this usage by societies and sports organisers gave them the broadest possible appeal, while carrying powerful associations of history and romance.

New Zealand Scots did not hesitate, though, to use Highland cultural emblems – tartan, pipes and dance – to project a sense of ethnicity, no matter their district of origin. During the late eighteenth century, a seismic shift in intellectual and cultural fashion completely altered public attitudes to Scottish Highlanders and their environment. Previously viewed as ugly and barren country, inhabited by a barbaric and pagan people, the Highlands were reinvented as a beautiful, spectacular and romantic landscape, the home of noble warriors. The 'myth' of the Highlands had been born. In the nineteenth century royal patronage gave an added boost to the increasingly pervasive fashion for Highland tours, Highland societies, Highland dress and Highland games. Highland culture came to be seen as a living remnant of a once national way of life, and Lowlanders, and the Scottish nation as a whole, adopted Highland emblems to maximise their distinctiveness from the neighbouring English culture which threatened to assimilate them.[139] It is, then, no surprise to find New Zealand's Scottish colonists demonstrating their Scottishness with Highland dress and music: they were displaying the fashion of the day. As Eric Richards notes, 'emigré Scots communities . . . typically maintained a pronounced Highland element, as if to emphasise a distinctiveness'. National societies attempted 'to resist the homogenisation of the Scots into a society which was being dominated by what were identified as specifically English forms'.[140]

The Caledonian games were self-consciously ethnic occasions. Certainly they included the running, leaping and novelty events general to all such occasions, but it was the skirl of the pipes and the sight of the kilt which gave these days their special flavour. In 1868 the Caledonian Society of Otago, when designing a games programme, decided to omit the blind wheelbarrow race and replace it with the Seann Triubhas, a Highland dance: the organisers' priorities clearly lay with the cultural events.[141] Many spectators, however, had different priorities, preferring athletics to cultural events. In 1899 the main attraction at Timaru's Caledonian games was the bicycle races, while in Dunedin the foot races became from 'year to year of greater relative importance', and were already the principal events by the 1880s.[142] Not all enjoyed the bagpipes: a

Pipers, marching along Princes Street, Dunedin, en route to the Caledonian games attract a crowd of onlookers. *ILLUSTRATED NEW ZEALAND NEWS*, 3 SEPTEMBER 1883, P. 8.

newspaper report of Dunedin's 1880 games noted that 'besides the Highland pipers, who promenaded the ground in all the pride of checkered tartan and bare knees, the Headquarters Band . . . was present to charm those who had a liking for more civilised music than that of the bagpipe'.[143]

The lesser popularity of the cultural events perhaps reflected the diversity of the audience. In 1874 the Dunedin Caledonian games attracted 'representatives of all the races and classes that compose our heterogeneous community. Of course North Britons were in a majority, but English and Irish were by no means scarce, and Germans, Scandinavians, French, Chinese, and Maoris, were all represented in the

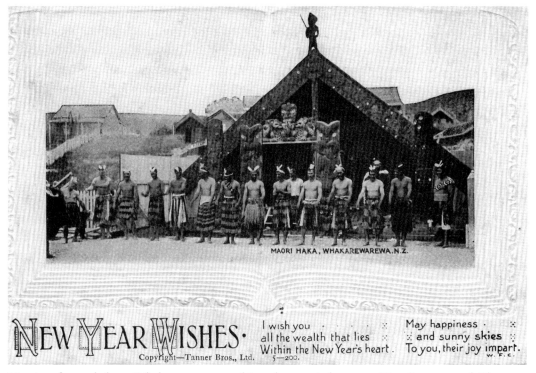

Maori perform a haka at Whakarewarewa on this early twentieth-century New Year postcard. Those New Zealanders who did not celebrate Christmas sometimes gave New Year cards and gifts. The haka provided a special native flavour to the card – the Maori 'war dance' was of great interest to late nineteenth-century Pakeha, who enjoyed seeing it performed at large New Year picnics and sports gatherings, and even at the Caledonian games. TANNER BROTHERS POSTCARD, GIVEN TO BERT AND PAULINE BY MOTHER, FROM THE AUTHOR'S COLLECTION.

crowd that thronged the green and grand stand.'[144] The Caledonian label was indeed a broad one – the Caledonian Society of Otago's membership list for 1884–85 included the prominent Otago Chinese name of Sew Hoy.[145] And in Wellington, one of the cultural displays at the Caledonian games of the 1860s was the haka performed by local Maori.[146] Certainly there were events varied enough to appeal to all.

Ironically, the widespread Caledonian games made the colonial New Year very different from the Scottish one. In Scotland such games took place not on a holiday, but on some convenient date in summer. In New Zealand, their position as a major organised event on Scotland's premier holiday, New Year, gave increased emphasis to the Scottishness of both games and holiday. The generally 'rational' and respectable activities of New Zealand residents presented a contrast to Scotland, where drinking was perhaps the most popular New Year sport.[147]

·ᴗ

Overall, the New Year holiday was a great success in nineteenth-century New Zealand. There may have been different ways of seeing in the New Year, but most New Zealanders, no matter what their ethnic or religious background, agreed that 1 January was a splendid day for a holiday, preferably spent outdoors in some enjoyable form of recreation. The nature of the holiday did vary somewhat from place to place and from year to year. One of the most striking features of New Year's Eve celebrations is their subdued nature whenever 1 January happened to fall on a Sunday. Nineteenth-century New Zealand had, like other Western societies, a remarkably sabbatarian culture – by today's standards, anyway. Sunday was a day of rest and worship and a day when even most non-churchgoers avoided work and any rowdy or frivolous form of recreation.[148] When New Year fell on a Sunday, the crowds of revellers who gathered on New Year's Eve were smaller and quieter, and tended to disappear home early to avoid profaning the Sabbath with loud revelry once midnight had struck. The 'New Year was ushered in with unusual quietness, there being but a moderate indulgence in the practice of those customs which prevail at the birth of a new year', reported the *Otago Witness* of Dunedin's 1888 celebrations. 'This was no doubt due to the fact that the year's natal day fell on a Sunday.'[149] In Hamilton, on 31 December 1881, many enjoyed the music of the Cambridge Brass Band playing out the old year and playing in the new. After midnight had struck, the band finished their performance with 'Auld Lang Syne' and the national anthem. But then the revelry swiftly halted. An 'attempt was made at three cheers for the band, and for the New Year, but as those present were convinced of the fact that it was Sunday morning, the call was not responded to, and was confined solely to the large man with the small voice with whom it originated'.[150] Likewise, when New Year fell on a Monday, fewer people gathered noisily in the streets on New Year's Eve, simply because it was Sunday and not the done thing. A good example comes from Lyttelton

Popular New Year activities in Dunedin included (from top left) picnics at the beach, New Year's Eve shopping, steamboat excursions, seeing in the New Year with band music, the Caledonian games and listening to the pipes. *ILLUSTRATED NEW ZEALAND HERALD*, 27 FEBRUARY 1880, P. 9.

in 1883: 'New Year's Eve falling on a Sunday, the town was comparatively quiet, but towards midnight a number of people began to congregate in the streets awaiting the hour of twelve'.[151] Once midnight arrived and the Sabbath was over, the fun and games could begin.

A holiday could not, of course, be taken on a Sunday, the weekly day of rest. In these cases, 1 January became just a regular Sunday, although the turning of the year provided a great sermon topic. Rather than having no holiday, most communities kept their great recreational holiday on Monday instead. Perhaps the best indication of the success of New Year as a holiday is that, even when it did not fall on Sunday, many people in larger towns took a two-day break from their work (possibly needing the second in order to recover from the exertions of the first). In Auckland, on Thursday, 2 January

1873, 'some few of the shopkeepers had opened their establishments for business, but there was no business done, and by noon, with exceptions which might be counted on one's fingers' ends, the whole had put up shutters and closed doors again. Employees went off to the races, or betook themselves to excursion trips, or retired to bars and bar parlors'.[152] As the years went on, fewer and fewer businesses remained open on 2 January in Auckland and some other towns. At the opposite end of the country, the residents of Invercargill observed Wednesday, 2 January 1878, 'as a close holiday in town, business being entirely suspended'. The main attraction was the second day of the Caledonian gathering, attended by about 2000 people, while many others went on railway excursions and picnics at the beach.[153]

In adopting the Scottish New Year holiday, and then adapting it to the midsummer call of the outdoors, New Zealanders had developed something all their own. By the end of the nineteenth century many New Zealand workers had four days of holiday over the Christmas and New Year period – Christmas Day, Boxing Day, New Year's Day and 2 January. Such extravagance was unthought of in Britain and Ireland at this time. As a local newspaper wrote for a 'home' audience in Britain:

> Holidays in the Australasian colonies are enjoyed with a thoroughness and *abandon* which even Englishmen, accustomed to reverence the leisure and joyousness of Christmas, can scarcely conceive. Our holidays here are more numerous than in England, and are participated in by all classes . . . During the few days between Boxing Day and New Year's Day little business is done. New Year's Day is another complete holiday; and it is not till the 3rd or 4th of January that life begins to flow again in its usual channels, and businessmen and politicians gird up their loins for the year's work which lies before them.[154]

⁀

CHAPTER THREE

Easter

Easter – the festival marking the death and resurrection of Jesus – was the most important event in the Christian year for New Zealand's nineteenth-century Anglicans and Catholics. Preparation, mourning and celebration combined to make up an extended period of special rituals. This chapter begins by exploring those religious rituals, unfamiliar to many today, yet central to the rationale behind the holiday. Keeping the rituals was not always easy in New Zealand. Good Friday may have been the most solemn day of the year for some people, but their neighbours were just as likely to spend it at a picnic or excursion, or to carry on working as usual: this holiday demonstrated most clearly the religious and cultural differences in nineteenth-century society.

But Easter traditions were never confined to explicitly religious ceremonies, and this chapter also pays attention to other aspects of the holiday. In the northern hemisphere, Easter was the great spring festival and many of its trimmings – Easter eggs, floral decorations and Easter bonnets – were symbols of new life. Migrants had difficulty adjusting such practices to the autumn setting of a colonial Easter, and never quite succeeded in making this a more seasonally appropriate holiday. They did, however, manage to keep up the old practice of outdoor recreation on Easter Monday. The sports, picnics and other community gatherings so popular at New Year featured again on Easter Monday, along with two distinctive colonial Easter activities – the hunting expedition and the Volunteer training camp.

The story of Easter in nineteenth-century New Zealand is, then, part of the complex story of the development of colonial culture. It sheds further light on nineteenth-century religion and recreation, and on the adjustment (successful or otherwise) of old-world practices to the new-world social and physical environment.

In twenty-first century New Zealand, it is not difficult to know when Easter is on the way. Hot cross buns and Easter eggs begin crowding supermarket shelves in the days, weeks and, it sometimes seems, months prior to the holiday. But for devout nineteenth-century Catholics and Anglicans the run-up to Easter had nothing to do with luxury foods. It meant the very opposite: self-denial. Easter marked the culmination of a period of preparation which began over six weeks earlier, on Ash Wednesday. That Wednesday was the first of the 40 days of Lent (Sundays were not counted among the 40 days, for they were always festive days). At the end of Lent came Holy Week, and then, finally, Easter Sunday. For some, particularly in southern Europe, Lent itself was preceded by carnival, a time of feasting and rowdy celebration prior to the period of fast and abstinence about to begin. In England and Ireland, the carnival was known as Shrovetide, although by the nineteenth century much of its celebration had died out. What remained was the custom which survives to this day of eating pancakes on Shrove Tuesday, the last opportunity before Lent to feast on eggs (which were forbidden, along with meat and cheese, until Henry VIII relaxed the Lenten fast in the 1500s to exclude meat only).[1]

The faithful imported their preparations for Easter to New Zealand, although it proved more difficult to recognise Lent in their new home. In Europe, Easter was the great spring festival and Lent fell at the end of winter (the name 'Lent' derives from 'lengthen' – it falls in the period when the days are starting to lengthen). It made sense to keep a fast during the time of year when food supplies were running low and to break that fast when spring, with its new life, arrived. In New Zealand, Lent came at the end of summer when food was abundant and it seemed more natural to celebrate the harvest than to avoid indulging in treats.

But it was the social environment rather than the physical which was most damaging to the keeping of Lent in New Zealand. Catholics – the denomination most wedded to the customs of Lent – formed a mere 14 per cent of the Pakeha population in nineteenth-century New Zealand. Anglicans, the other keepers of Lent, formed a more substantial 40 per cent. Still, of those Anglican adherents, many were not frequent churchgoers, and even the diligent Anglican churchgoers tended, in the first few decades of European settlement, to be suspicious of anything that suggested a Catholic style of ritual. Moreover, many of nineteenth-century New Zealand's more devout

Christians were Presbyterian, Baptist or Congregationalist, and they paid no heed to Easter, let alone Lent. Methodists, some 10 per cent of the population, generally recognised Easter, but not Lent.

Catholic and Anglican clergy had difficulty persuading their congregations to keep Lent faithfully when they were surrounded by others who ignored it. This was particularly the case in Otago, where Presbyterians greatly outnumbered Anglicans and Catholics. Archdeacon Edwards, who had been in Otago since the 1850s, told the 1874 Synod of the Anglican Diocese of Otago and Southland that it was 'very painful to him to see so little regard paid to the holy season of Lent in Dunedin. Unfortunately, during that season a great many parties were given, and the annual races were then held.' He thought it 'the duty of the members to set their faces against unnecessary festivities during that season'.[2]

Little had changed by 1898, when the clergy of St Matthew's Anglican Church, Dunedin, wrote a circular letter encouraging their parishioners to recognise Lent, 'a season of self-discipline (commonly called fasting), penitence, and special devotion'. The Anglican Church had, the letter went on, 'no rules for Lenten observance', but made it clear that this was a time for self-contemplation, for 'overhauling' body, soul and spirit. 'Your body may be all the better, and the more expressive of a beautiful soul by some self-discipline – by indulging the appetites less, by abstaining from unhealthy excitement – any act by which you can feel you have won a mastery over the flesh, is a Lenten discipline which the Church invites you to perform.' Vicar William Curzon-Siggers and curate Hugh Leach offered, in addition to their usual busy schedule, special Lenten services on Wednesday and Friday evenings.[3] Catholics, likewise, had plenty of opportunities to meditate and 'overhaul' themselves during Lent. At Dunedin's St Joseph's Cathedral, for example, during Lent in 1884 they could attend, in addition to the usual services, 'an instruction on each Monday, Tuesday, and Wednesday evening, with Benediction of the Most Holy Sacrament on Thursday, and the Way of the Cross on Friday'.[4]

What sort of 'unhealthy excitement' did pious colonial Anglicans and Catholics abstain from during Lent? Fasting, in remembrance of Jesus' 40 days in the desert without food, seems to have been the most commonly kept practice, although even that was not widely discussed. By the nineteenth century the 'fast' did not mean avoidance of all food, just the most luxurious kind: meat. Most practising Catholics, and some Anglicans, kept a similar fast every Friday. Those who could obtain fish simply ate that

Fishermen at Island Bay, Wellington. Many fishermen there were Italian Catholics, for whom Lent had both personal and professional significance. Lent gave a boost to the fishing industry, with devout Catholics and Anglicans replacing meat with fish. In seventeenth-century England one of King Charles I's arguments for continuing the Lent ban on meat was that it helped defend the realm by fostering the fisheries and thereby shipping and the navy. F-56420-1/2, ALEXANDER TURNBULL LIBRARY, WELLINGTON.

instead of meat. L. D. Nathan & Co., Jewish merchants in Auckland, catered for the needs of well-to-do fasters. In 1895, under the heading 'Lent', they advertised a variety of canned and boxed fish on sale 'during the season', including 'American Cod, Shetland Ling, Salmon, Lobsters, Herrings, Oysters etc'.[5] Keeping the Lenten fast would have been a more serious matter for those without ready access to fish, such as farm workers, who generally ate three meals of meat every day.

The church could be flexible about the fast, taking account of special circumstances. In 1890 Dunedin's Catholic Bishop, Patrick Moran, announced that the Pope had granted a dispensation from the Lenten fast in areas where influenza prevailed. Those who took advantage of this dispensation should, instead, 'devote themselves to pious works, be assiduous in the holy practice of prayer, frequent the sacraments, and be more than usually generous to the poor and needy'.[6] In 1851 Vicesimus Lush, Anglican vicar at Howick, Auckland, allowed his family to break the fast for a more light-hearted reason – his son Charlie's second birthday. 'Though it were Lent', he recorded in his diary, 'we had to commemorate the event a stewed beef steak and baked plum pudding: and after dinner a glass of wine between all the children over which they drank one another's health.'[7]

Lush was not willing, though, to be frivolous in public during Lent. In the 1870s, while vicar at Thames, he refused to attend a ball given in honour of a visit from the governor, 'partly because it was Lent – partly because we thought it would be very mixed: as it was'.[8] He was dismayed, too, when he discovered that the Thames schools had a holiday on the first day of Lent, Ash Wednesday, not for any religious purpose, but to allow the children to attend the races. 'This', he wrote, 'is a great Colonial evil – the making of holiday on Good Friday and Ash Wednesday.'[9] Anglican clergy regularly spoke out against racing and parties during Lent, apparently with little success. But they made no public comment about another activity traditionally avoided during Lent: sex. The St Matthew's Lenten pamphlet, with its reference to 'indulging the appetites less', probably referred to all bodily appetites, including the carnal. It was not common to refer to sexual matters in print during the Victorian era, except in veiled language such as this. Caroline Abraham, wife of the Anglican Archdeacon of Waitemata, apparently felt guilty for simply enjoying her husband's company during Lent in 1857. Charles, who had broken his arm, was unable to work as usual, and although Caroline was deeply concerned about his recovery, as she wrote to her friend Sophia Marriott she had rather enjoyed the last few weeks of very quiet time with my dear Husband . . . it has been very pleasant to have him to tend – and to read and write for and take care of and to have so much of his company – and such long long undisturbed morn[ing] readings. Almost too pleasant for Lent.[10]

Charles Bowden, vicar of St Mary's Anglican Church in the Dunedin suburb of Mornington, gave his parishioners some practical suggestions for Lent of 1897. The 'true object' of Lent, he noted, was 'to leave some permanent spiritual impression on our lives, to help us after Lent is over to continue to lead our lives on a higher level of repentance and self-sacrifice than before'. He did not ask them 'to make frantic exertions' – a request like this, he realised, many would simply 'put aside as impossible'. It was 'within the power of all', he believed, to attend a weekly service, come more frequently to communion, and 'read over on your knees every Friday at least, the fifty-first Psalm'. Bowden also suggested a little self-denial with respect to the usual 'harmless pleasure' of life, such as smoking one pipe a day instead of three, or reading 'some good biography or book of travel' instead of novels. And should any of the St Mary's parishioners suffer from 'some besetting sin or weakness', this was the time to 'make more strenuous efforts than before' to fight it. Any savings resulting from the self-denial of Lent could be given to his favourite cause, the Melanesian Mission.[11]

Few of the St Mary's congregation gave up any very extravagant pleasures, judging by the £1 3s 1d they placed in the Melanesian Mission Box during Lent, although this was a considerable increase on the 11s 7d received from 'self-denial offerings' the previous year. Five shillings of the 1897 amount came from a woman who gave up the daily newspaper. Bowden noted that he would have found this 'the hardest piece of self-denial almost of anything, and I expect most men would agree with me'.[12] If late nineteenth-century Mornington Anglicans are typical, it seems that most New Zealand churchgoers of this period did not go in for extremes of asceticism during Lent.

One activity traditionally avoided during Lent was marriage. It involved, after all, several activities frowned upon during the season: celebration, sex and in many cases feasting as well. (Here lies the origin of the popular Easter wedding: after two months when weddings were frowned upon, many couples sped to the altar as soon as the clergy permitted.) In 1893 a *New Zealand Herald* columnist reported one clergyman

A colonial Irish Catholic bride. Rose Savage married Ned Cain in rural Victoria, Australia, in 1890. Like many of the rural Irish, they married in February – at Shrovetide, just before Lent began. Rose's young brother Michael, whom she had raised after their mother's death, later came to New Zealand and became one of this country's best-loved prime ministers. MS-PAPERS-1361-5-01, MICHAEL J. SAVAGE COLLECTION, ALEXANDER TURNBULL LIBRARY, WELLINGTON.

had refused to marry, on the grounds that it was Holy Week (the week leading up to Easter), some couples who had travelled from Waikato to Auckland at the beginning of the Easter holidays. 'Mercutio' had little time for such a ban. 'If there is anything holy', he wrote, 'I should have thought it was the holy bonds of matrimony, but the parson evidently thought it would never do to have too much joy.'[13] New Zealand Anglicans seem to have had little respect for the Lent ban on weddings and many vicars were less strict than this unidentified Auckland priest. The Dunedin and Invercargill marriage registers show that Lent was as popular as any other period of the year for Anglican weddings, although marriages were a little less common in Holy Week than in other weeks of the year.[14] Catholics, though, were more diligent than Anglicans in respecting Lent by avoiding marriage – similar scrutiny of Catholic marriage registers in Otago and Southland showed very few marriages during Lent, and only one during Holy Week. One day which did prove popular for Catholic marriages was Shrove Tuesday – the final opportunity for celebration before Lent began.[15] Shrovetide was the favoured time of year for marriage in rural Ireland, and it seems that many migrant Irish Catholics continued this practice in their new homeland.[16]

The marriage statistics suggest that New Zealand Catholics and, to a lesser extent, Anglicans, took Holy Week rather more seriously than the rest of Lent. For Catholics, though, even the week before Holy Week – Passion Week – held a special sobriety. Colonial Irish Catholics usually celebrated St Patrick's Day with vigour. In 1875, when the saint's day fell during Passion Week, Dunedin's Hibernian Society postponed their usual St Patrick's Day celebrations, as any festivities would be 'deemed out of place' in that week. Instead they attended communion together on the Sunday after St Patrick's Day, and reserved their usual conviviality until the holy season had ended. Reverend William Coleman 'recommended all Irish Catholics to join with the Hibernian Society in honouring Ireland's Patron Saint in the manner proposed, on Sunday next, and to abstain from any public demonstration during Passion Week'.[17] Anglicans paid less attention to Passion Week than Catholics, and it may have been his Irish background which led former Anglican vicar William Minchin to take great offence at the holding of races during the Passion Week of 1864 in the Hutt Valley. This, he claimed, might cause 'the Judgment of a slighted Saviour, and a justly offended God, [to] break forth on a guilty neighbourhood'.[18]

Holy Week may have been a time to avoid festivity, but Catholic churches had many interesting activities on offer for the devout.[19] In 1873 Jessie Mackay, newly arrived in Dunedin from Scotland, described the wonders of Easter at St Joseph's Cathedral in a breathless letter to her sister:

> We have just got over the easter time and the offices and ceremonies of Holy Week
> were quite new to us altogether there was the office of the tenebrae three night and
> the holy thursday there was high Mass and the blessing of the Oils a beautifull [sic] cer-
> emony then on good Friday there was the Mass of the presanctified on Saturday there
> was the blessing of the Paschal candle there was six priests all the week the services
> were all sung and there was two or three of the priests sing magnificently.[20]

In her native Banffshire, where Catholics were few, Mackay did not have the opportunity to attend such ceremonies. But as the church grew in size and staff in urban areas of New Zealand, Catholics could observe Holy Week with a wealth of ritual.

The Holy Week ceremonies began on Palm Sunday, the Sunday before Easter, which recalled Jesus' arrival in Jerusalem, when crowds threw palm branches before him as he rode by on a donkey. In 1886 the Catholic churches of Auckland observed 'the time-honoured custom of distributing the blessed palms to the faithful', when the priest blessed the palms and the congregation took them home, where they served as a reminder of the season.[21] The evening office of Tenebrae began on Holy Wednesday and was repeated on Thursday and Friday. The Catholic weekly, the *New Zealand Tablet*, described this service:

> The word 'tenebrae' means 'darkness,' and is used of this office because it was formerly recited in the darkness of the night, or in the darkness of the catacombs. The choice of psalms to be said, the mode of recital, and the sorrowful music . . . all strike the mind and show that the Church wishes now no thought but that of Jesus crucified.[22]

It was the lighting at Tenebrae which achieved the most dramatic effect. After each psalm, one of the fifteen special candles in front of the altar was extinguished until only one remained. As the priests sang the 'Benedictus' the six altar candles were put out. The remaining special candle was then hidden, sending the church into complete darkness.

Holy or 'Maundy' Thursday commemorated Jesus' last supper with his disciples, the origin of the Christian ritual of communion. During mass in Catholic churches, the priest consecrated an extra host, which was laid aside in a special container, the sepulchre, to be released again on Good Friday. The faithful came to adore this host, and devotional associations kept watch over it. Typically, at St Joseph's Cathedral, Dunedin, in 1888,

> watch was maintained before the sepulchre during the day by the members of the Confraternity of Our Lady of Perpetual Succour and the Sodality of the Children of Mary, and during the entire night by the members of the Confraternity of the Holy Family. Hymns were sung and prayers repeated at intervals, and the sound of the men's voices in the depths of the night was particularly impressive and solemn.[23]

Thursday also saw the stripping or disguising of all ornament from the church, in preparation for the solemnity of Good Friday. One place alone remained decorated: the altar of repose, a side altar where the sacred host and sepulchre lay. Whatever items the altar displayed shone out amidst the sobriety. The *Tablet* described the vivid effect at St Joseph's in Dunedin in 1897, when 'the altar of repose was beautifully decorated with a profusion of flowers and candles, affording a striking contrast to the high altar which was stripped of its ornaments and covered with the draperies of mourning'.[24]

•➤

Good Friday, which recalls the crucifixion of Jesus, was for Catholics and Anglicans the most solemn day of the year. The sobriety of Lent, which increased during Holy Week, culminated in the ceremonies of Good Friday. In large Catholic churches these could be quite involved, as at St Benedict's, Auckland, in 1896. At the morning service, a procession led the special host, consecrated the previous day, to the altar for the 'mass of the pre-sanctified'. The congregation also took part in the 'adoration of the Cross'. Jesus had died in the afternoon, so at that time of day the St Benedict's faithful marked his death by performing the Stations of the Cross, ending with 'the blessing of the congregation with a fragment of the True Cross, which all present devoutly kissed at the altar rails'. The evening service included 'an impressive sermon on the Passion delivered with great force and eloquence' by Father Kehoe, a recitation of 'the Seven Dolours of Mary', and, once again, a blessing with a relic of 'the True Cross'.[25] The removal or disguise of all the usual statues and ornaments promoted the congregation's concentration on the great symbol of the day, the cross, and appropriate music added to the solemnity.

Anglicans, like Catholics, held special services on Good Friday, frequently attracting large congregations. Although less ornate than the Catholic ceremonies, these, too, included solemn music and prayers, and many Anglican churches draped their altar and other furnishings in black. During the late nineteenth century the 'three hours service' became popular in Anglican churches. The service began at noon and ended at three, noted in the Bible as the hour of Jesus' death, and concentrated on his final sufferings. A typical example took place in 1884 at St Paul's Cathedral, Auckland. Reverend William Jervois 'gave a series of devotional addresses on the seven last words [of Jesus], interspersed with hymns and prayers . . . a goodly number were present during the three hours, coming and going during the singing of the hymns. This service was throughout most impressive and devout.'[26] At Temuka, in 1892, Reverend Thomas Hamilton used the latest technology to illustrate his Good Friday message. After the evening service he showed 'magic lantern views of Our Lord's Passion and Crucifixion' to accompany his talk on the topic of the day.[27]

While a 'goodly number' of people attended the solemn services of Good Friday, others enjoyed a day of recreation or simply ignored the holiday. These differing Good Friday practices clearly demonstrate the religious and cultural differences in colonial New Zealand. Presbyterians, Congregationalists and Baptists did not recognise Easter as a religious holiday during the nineteenth century. The New Zealand Presbyterian newspaper, the *Outlook*, explained their thinking in 1899:

> We do not observe Good Friday as a holy day. We go on the footing that it is exceed-
> ingly dangerous to invent religious rites or observe holy days other than those which
> the divine word has prescribed . . . . In order that we may avoid all impious scandal it is
> well to remember not only on Good Friday but on all the days that the Son of God died
> for our sins on the cursed tree.

Conservative Presbyterians were strongly opposed to Catholic forms of ritual, decrying also the 'stealthy methods used by advanced ritualists in the Church of England to propagate their views'. While prepared to admit that the crucifixion of Jesus was 'the greatest event that has ever occurred on this earth' and 'the central fact of all history', they could not bring themselves to be associated with such rituals as the religious observance of Good Friday.[28] By this period some more liberal Presbyterians were starting to recognise the worth of the Christian year, but they did not overcome conservative opposition until 1931, when the Presbyterian Church of New Zealand officially recommended the religious observance of Good Friday.[29]

Methodists had a more moderate approach to Easter and their individual practice varied widely. Thomas Ferens, who migrated from Durham to Otago in 1848, was rather surprised at the extent of Easter observance at the Wesleyan mission at Waikouaiti, which he joined as a teacher. Although the devout Ferens treated Easter Sunday as something special ('the thoughts of Christ and his resurrection cheered my heart greatly', he wrote in his diary) he was clearly unaccustomed to keeping

OPPOSITE AND ABOVE: These two photographs of the old St Paul's Anglican Cathedral, Dunedin, in 1895 demonstrate the contrast between Lent and Easter. During Lent there were no flowers and the altar was covered with a simple cloth and bore only a plain cross and Bible. Some churches went further and were draped in black for Good Friday. On Easter Day, a beautiful cloth covered the altar, and there were candles in abundance. Although there was not a huge display of flowers, there was plenty of greenery, particularly around the pulpit. S06-518F AND S06-518E, HOCKEN COLLECTIONS, UARE TAOKA O HAKENA, UNIVERSITY OF OTAGO.

Good Friday as a holiday. 'We all agreed, not to go and work, as the Maories would not!!' he exclaimed. In later years, running a sheep station in North Otago, he paid no heed to Good Friday.[30] James Watkin, the first Wesleyan missionary in the south of New Zealand, had a very different attitude to Easter. It was he who had taught Kai Tahu at Waikouaiti to respect Good Friday, noting that he observed the day 'as at home, by abstinence from labour and food, and by religious services as at home'.[31] In 1874 the *New Zealand Wesleyan* described the position of Methodists, which fell between Catholics and Anglicans on one hand, and Presbyterians and Baptists on the other: 'Methodists do not object to the religious observance of Good Friday; but they condemn not their fellow-Christians who choose to make it a season of recreation'.[32]

Migrants from England and Ireland could be taken aback by the lack of respect for their religious holidays in New Zealand. As the *Otago Daily Times* warned before Good Friday of 1864, 'the holiday is less strictly observed here than it is at home; and there are various announcements of excursions'.[33] In rural districts Easter frequently passed by without notice, and those who worked for others could not always keep Good Friday as they wished. Oamaru woman Susie Sumpter attended the Good Friday Anglican service in 1862 – her husband George would have liked to join her but instead spent the day digging potatoes for his employer.[34] Likewise, Frederic Otto, newly arrived from Germany, saw no sign of the familiar 'Green Thursday and Good Friday festivities' while working as a farm labourer in Mangere. Instead he 'cleaned the cattle's water trough (that was a nice job for Good Friday)'.[35]

Such failure to keep Easter as a holiday was not confined to rural districts. Anglican Charlotte Godley, who with her husband, Canterbury founder John Godley, visited Dunedin in 1850, was shocked to discover that even the religious Cargills, leaders of the Otago settlement, did not commemorate Easter. 'I should think them a very nice family', she wrote to her mother, 'but it seems strange to be with people who do not even know when Easter Sunday is; though Mrs Cargill calls herself Episcopalian, all the others are Free Kirk'.[36] It was, of course, easy enough for those unaccustomed to keeping Easter to let it slip by without notice, because the date shifted from year to year, and Easter Day could fall on any date from 22 March to 25 April. To most onlookers, there was no obvious pattern to this date, which marked the first Sunday following the first full moon on or after 21 March, the northern hemisphere's spring equinox. In 1853 the Otago newspaper began printing a weekly almanac that noted significant dates such as Easter, in response to an embarrassing incident when 'owing to an inadvertency' the day named for the Anniversary Fair, a stock auction, 'happen[ed] to fall on Good Friday'. The organisers delayed the fair for a week once the 'inadvertency' was discovered.[37]

Other New Zealanders cared less about the possible offence to Catholics and Anglicans by desecrating their sacred day, and some deliberately demonstrated their disregard for others' religious sensibilities. The problem lay with keeping Good Friday as a public holiday. In England, Good Friday was a common-law holiday, and government offices, banks and many other operations in New Zealand followed the English precedent and closed for the day. By the mid-1860s even Dunedin, least English of New Zealand towns, generally kept holiday on Good Friday. But, throughout New Zealand, many of those on holiday were not practising Anglicans and Catholics. These people naturally seized this rare opportunity to enjoy a little rest and recreation, commonly with private parties and picnics. Dunedin merchant James Kilgour described the occasion to his brother in 1867: 'Yesterday was good Friday which is kept here by all the Folks we had Jessie Alexander & her Husband Mr Hannah & Helen Alexander up at Roslyn'.[38] Jack Fowler, a Dunedin bootmaker and a good Baptist, enjoyed an excursion on the Otago Central Railway with his future wife Jeannie Broome on Good Friday 1888; two years later he spent the Easter holidays digging up his garden 'sufficient to plant 75 strawberry plants and some 150 cabbages'.[39] In Wellington, on Good Friday 1865, the 'harbour was covered with pleasure boats, and on the Hutt Road many happy families, and cosy couples might have been seen quietly jogging out to the country to witness the sports held in Dr Taylor's paddock, for the amusement of the Johnsonville school children'.[40]

Although much Good Friday recreation was private in nature, some organisations arranged holiday gatherings for their members, and among them were Protestant churches. Some, it appears, did so to show in a very public way that they did not recognise this 'Papist' religious occasion. In 1873 Vicesimus Lush, Anglican vicar at Thames, was disturbed by

> a party of men and boys and girls with a band playing and flags flying passing our Church (shortly before the bell began ringing) on their way to Parawai for a pic-nic, cricketing, &c. It so happened that they returned more noisily even than they started as my congregation were assembling for the evening service. Whether they *timed* their starting and returning so as to clash as much as possible with the 'English Church' I know not.

The picnic party were 'Israelite Christians' (and I can only echo Lush's comment, 'whoever *they* are'); meanwhile the local Primitive Methodists held a soirée just along the road from St George's Church. These events made Lush 'painfully sensible of the divisions in Christendom'.[41]

In 1885 a Dunedin newspaper columnist noted that on Good Friday 'the Blueskin Presbyterians commemorated their Redeemer's crucifixion by a picnic, and the

Dunedin Lyceumites – not to be beaten in liberalism by the orthodox – celebrated the same event by a "concert, farce, and ball"'.[42] The 'Lyceumites' were the Dunedin Freethought Association. Nineteenth-century New Zealand's most significant secularists, freethinkers saw it as their duty to 'weaken the hold of the church on society'.[43] Their Good Friday activities were undoubtedly designed to desecrate the religious holiday. The motives of the Blueskin (now better known as Waitati) Presbyterians are less clear. Perhaps, like Auckland's Beresford Street Congregational Church members, who gathered in large numbers for Good Friday steamer excursions and picnics, or the Primitive Methodists of Te Henui, Taranaki, who held their children's picnic on Good Friday for at least 40 years, they were simply taking advantage of an available holiday.[44]

Whether intended or not, such events did cause offence to devout Catholics and Anglicans. In 1882 Dunedin Anglican Bishop Nevill protested against a concert to be given by the Invercargill Band on Good Friday. As he explained, it could 'hardly fail to grate harshly upon the feelings' of those Christians who 'specially devote themselves' during Holy Week to commemorating their Lord's sufferings that, 'at the hour which commemorates the quiet of the tomb, an entertainment should be given'.[45] Likewise, in 1887 the *Tablet*, mouthpiece of Dunedin Catholic Bishop Moran and always outspoken on the deficiencies of government-run schools, raged against a Good Friday 'entertainment' to be held by a Southland school. Good Friday, stated the paper, 'is observed as one of penitential solemnity not only by Catholics, but by members of the Church of England, and all except those who openly scoff at Christianity, should disapprove of its being made an occasion of festivity'. That such festivities were indulged in by 'the extreme atheistical mob of continental Europe . . . with the express intention of outraging Christianity, makes it still more flagrant that like doings should distinguish our Government system of education, and brands this with the common mark of atheism and profanity'. The occasion would be a 'public insult to the memory of their Redeemer, and yet we conclude, they are for the most part the children of people who call themselves Christians'.[46]

Sometimes the organisers of Good Friday activities took note of such criticism. In 1879 Felix Goodfellow of Auckland's Star Hotel announced 'an athletic carnival on a large scale' to be held on Good Friday and the following day. A flurry of complaints followed. An anonymous Anglican, claiming to speak for 'a large portion of this community', noted that 'such a project is exceedingly distasteful to me. Accustomed, as we have been from our earliest years, to regard the day as one of the most sacred in the Christian calendar, and as one which calls to mind the most solemn and tender thoughts, we cannot but feel that sports on such a day would be out of place.' Goodfellow expressed some surprise at the response: 'I had no idea that I would give rise to any feeling for or against, as I have been accustomed to attend the Lillie Bridge meeting on that day, which is perhaps the largest of the kind held in England'. Nevertheless, reluctant to alienate potential customers, he altered the dates 'at considerable inconvenience and loss to myself'.[47]

It is clear, though, that there were many people who had no objection to Good Friday sports. The following year a large crowd gathered at Orakei, having heard that local Maori were to offer a series of races and sports. They went away disappointed: there were 'no preparations for any amusement' because 'the clergymen and other chiefs were opposed to it from religious motives, it being Good Friday'.[48] At Middlemarch, in 1899, the local Caledonian Society arranged Good Friday bicycle sports, to be followed by a concert and ball. Although the local newspaper columnist published his dismay at this lack of 'respect for the sacredness of that day of all days in the year', finding it 'a disgrace to the district', he represented a minority view.[49] Good Friday, in New Zealand, would always hold different meanings – a holy day for some, for others simply a holiday.

• ﻌ

Easter Day, the day when Christians celebrate the resurrection of Jesus, brought less controversy than Good Friday. For Catholics, Anglicans and Methodists this was a day of great joy, the highlight of the Christian year. They were unlikely to be much bothered by the lively activities of other members of the community that could cause so much upset on Good Friday, the day of mourning. Those Protestants who opposed the religious celebration of Easter were great keepers of the Sabbath, and as Easter Day always fell on Sunday they were too busy keeping their own weekly religious ceremonies to disturb others. Desecrating this 'Papist' festival would have meant desecrating the Sabbath, something good Presbyterians and Baptists tried very hard to avoid.

Easter services in the earlier years of European settlement were generally simple. In the early 1860s Catherine Dewe of Tokomairiro, South Otago, attended her local

Anglican church on Easter Sunday, and sometimes Good Friday as well. Her diary reveals that these services differed in only one respect from those of regular Sundays: on Easter Sunday the congregation sang Easter hymns instead of their usual psalms. Her father, a lay reader, probably conducted the service. Communion had to wait until an ordained priest visited (in 1861 there was a flurry of activity on the weekend after Easter, when the Bishop's visit created an opportunity for communion, baptism, confirmation and Catherine Dewe's marriage).[50] As Bosco Peters notes, most early Anglican colonists were low church in theology, that is, they preferred their religion plain, without too much in the way of complicated ritual: 'They were usually conservative and pragmatic, focusing on getting established in a new land. After the first generation, however, the prospering colony began to look for Victorian luxuries in church as well as home.'[51]

The *Book of Common Prayer*, guide to religious practice for Anglicans, required all parishioners to take communion at least three times a year, one of which should be at Easter. But many Anglicans were reluctant to take communion. This was not because they did not value the sacrament, but because they valued it so much that they thought themselves unworthy to participate. This was probably the result of generations of preaching by Anglican clergy, who 'in their efforts to encourage their flocks to prepare more carefully for receiving the sacrament, ended up by discouraging them from receiving it at all'.[52] In nineteenth-century England, many lay people saw communion as a rite for the dying, delaying participation due to 'a fear of its power, and more particularly a fear of incurring eternal damnation through unworthy reception'.[53]

Vestry books, which record the number of people attending church and also those taking communion, show that in many New Zealand parishes Anglicans were reluctant partakers of communion at all times, including Easter. At St Mark's, Balclutha, 127 people attended the services on Easter Sunday 1882 but only fifteen took communion; at St Peter's, Queenstown, 128 people attended the 1890 Easter services, with only fourteen communicants.[54] George Sumpter of Oamaru, a most devout man, displays the serious approach to communion that may have been typical of colonial Anglicans. He first took communion in 1862, aged 26 years, recording in his diary: 'Stayed to the communion for the first time. A most solemn service. God grant that through Christ I may not have partaken it unworthily sinful though I be & may I be more & more anxious to do my duty.'[55]

But if many Anglicans failed to take communion, they did attend Easter services in large numbers – only harvest thanksgiving, and in a few places Christmas, could attract so many people across the church threshold. Typically, as on Easter Day of 1872, the

Anglican churches of Auckland were 'crowded with attentive congregations, on the occasion of one of the greatest of the sacred festivals of the year'.[56] It was not only numbers that made for the success of Easter services, but the enthusiasm of the congregations. Those attending St Paul's Anglican Cathedral in Auckland for Easter 1874 participated 'with a heartiness and good will calculated to create a warmth of holy joy in the hearts of the congregation'.[57] This was not a passing phase – Easter services had become even more popular by the turn of the century. In 1897 an Auckland newspaper commented that 'while we see many old customs and time-honoured observances fast becoming obsolete, if not already extinct, Easter, the oldest of ecclesiastical feasts, still holds its own and defies the ravages of time. Indeed . . . the observance of Easter Day is becoming more vigorous with age.' Anglican and Catholic services in the city were so crowded that some had been turned away, and, in Auckland at least, Anglicans were clearly losing their reluctance to take communion, with record turnouts, such as the 250 who took the sacrament on Easter Day at All Saints' Church in Ponsonby.[58]

As at Christmas, special music and decorations added to the appeal of Easter Day services, and by the late nineteenth century they had become major features of the Easter festival in Anglican churches. Old traditions remained popular – in 1881, all four Easter services at St Matthew's Anglican Church, Auckland, 'were commenced by singing the old Easter Hymn'.[59] This hymn, 'Jesus Christ is risen today, Alleluia . . .', was one of just a handful of hymns appearing in the traditional Anglican psalm book of the early nineteenth century; it remains perhaps the most popular Easter hymn to this day. By the late nineteenth century most churches had reasonably competent choirs, and in the larger centres they made significant contributions to the festival. At St John's Anglican Cathedral, Napier, 'the musical portion of the service was excellent' at the crowded morning service on Easter Day 1896. The choir processed in and out singing appropriate hymns, and also tackled plain chant canticles, an Easter anthem, 'Why seek ye the living among the dead?', and Tours' version of the 'Credo'. At the evening service, again crowded, Tours' 'Magnificat' and 'Nunc Dimittis' were 'capitally sung', also the 'beautiful Easter anthem "On the first day of the week they came to the sepulchre"', Rupert Gibson 'taking the tenor solo most capably'. During the offering they sang the 'glorious "Hallelujah Chorus," from the "Messiah".'[60] Congregations blessed with particularly talented soloists could enjoy something really special on Easter Day. At Holy Trinity Anglican Church, Gisborne, for Easter 1890, 'Miss Holroyd sang Handel's beautiful "I know that my Redeemer liveth" from the Messiah. Miss Holroyd was in splendid voice, and her execution of the piece was really very fine, and was much appreciated.'[61] This Handel aria, like the 'Hallelujah Chorus', became an Easter favourite.

Catholics, too, made special efforts to present fine music for Easter. While the Gisborne Anglicans enjoyed Miss Holroyd's Easter 1890 aria, their Catholic neighbours had the opportunity to hear Miss Lonergan sing 'He wipes the tear from every eye' and Mrs Hennessy's 'exquisite' performance of 'Tantum Ergo', a 'very rare and choice piece of music'.[62] In another typical example, at one of the 1893 Easter services at Oamaru, the choir 'added greatly by their beautiful singing to the joyful sanctity of the day' with a 'most commendable' performance of Webbe's Mass.[63] And like Anglicans, Catholics attended church in large numbers at Easter for the biggest services of the year. In 1893 at St Joseph's Catholic Cathedral, Dunedin, the attendance at 'all the ceremonies of the holy season . . . was strikingly numerous . . . The fervour of the people throughout the whole week was such as must have given joy to the Bishop and his clergy'. Crowds attended the Easter morning services and 'in the evening at Vespers even standing room in the church could hardly be found'. There was one striking difference from many Anglican services – at the Easter morning mass 'almost the whole congregation received Holy Communion'.[64]

Catholics, like Anglicans, were expected by their church to take communion at Easter, and many did so. In Oamaru, nearly 200 people took communion on Easter morning 1884, the priest trusting that 'all who had not already fulfilled their Easter obligations' would do so over the next fortnight. The *Tablet*'s colourful report of the service captured the fervour of the occasion: 'A bright sunny day; a large body of worshippers; better still, a crowd of communicants; the Church singing aloud her "Alleluias" in pure gladness of heart; the dear Lord present on our altar, and in the very embrace of so many of His creatures; – what more could be to make a joyous Easter?'[65] Catholics in late nineteenth-century Ireland were renowned for their piety.[66] New Zealand's Catholic Church had a strong Irish identity, and Ireland's nineteenth-century 'devotional revolution' came to this country via migrant priests and laity, and revivalist missions such as those of the Redemptorists. Although New Zealand Catholics attended church less diligently than Irish Catholics, a significant proportion practised their religion with great piety.[67] Catholic Easter ritual in New Zealand both reflected and fostered this late nineteenth-century devotional fervour.

•ꙅ

The congregation of St Peter's Anglican Church, Caversham, Dunedin, could enjoy an impressive abundance of late summer flowers for Easter, as this undated photograph reveals. The altar cloths bear the traditional Easter texts, 'Christ is risen indeed', 'Alleluia', and 'Christ the first fruits'. NEG E6858/25, HOCKEN COLLECTIONS, UARE TAOKA O HAKENA, UNIVERSITY OF OTAGO.

One aspect of Easter ritual in New Zealand could not help but differ from the traditions of Europe: the decorations, which became ever more widespread and ornate in Anglican and Catholic churches in the late Victorian period, could not include the spring blooms which were such a feature of Easter in the northern hemisphere. To migrants from the other side of the world an autumn Easter seemed as out of place as a summer Christmas or New Year. Helen Mills enjoyed the very pretty decorations at Marton's Anglican Church in 1885 but, as she wrote to her mother in England, 'it looked so odd to see all the late summer & autumn flowers for Easter. I thought of St James & wished to be there.'[68]

Flowers could be scarce in autumn, and finding suitable blooms was a challenge, especially in the north of the country (plants flowered later in the south) or if the season were dry. Chrysanthemums were a godsend to decorators and became the main feature of Easter displays in many churches. In 1886 Emily Harris of Nelson noted that 'Easter this year is so late that the chrysanthemums are well out & the decorations in the church in consequence looked unusually lovely'.[69] Lilies were another popular choice. The lily, associated with several mother goddesses in ancient times, was linked with Mary, mother of Jesus, in Christian tradition. *Lilium candidum*, one of the oldest cultivars of lily, has the common name Madonna lily and its pure white blooms are a symbol of purity. The lily is also associated with Jesus because of its suggestions of virtue, and because he referred to the flower in one of his parables. In the northern hemisphere, lilies could not feature at Easter until the introduction of a new Japanese variety, *Lilium longiflorum*, during the nineteenth century, but New Zealanders could choose from a variety of late-flowering lilies for Easter decorations.[70]

Some church decorators resorted to dried or artificial flowers. At All Saints' Anglican Church, Auckland, for Easter 1893, 'the lack of fresh flowers was amply supplied by immortelles', a variety of daisy which dried particularly well. The effect was 'beautiful indeed'.[71] Instead of resorting to such measures, many churches overcame the shortage of flowers by relying instead on greenery for most of their Easter decorations. Native plants came to the fore, partly because they were readily available and partly because of the attraction they held for the increasing number of New Zealanders born in this land and for migrants who began to identify more closely with their new country as time passed. 'The exquisite taste displayed in the management of the flowers, ferns, and variegated flax of the colony was in perfect keeping and harmony with the Easter festival', read a newspaper report in 1887 on the decorations at Sacred Heart Catholic Church in Ponsonby, Auckland. The paper also approved of the Easter decorations at Auckland's St Matthew's Anglican Church in 1892. They were 'of a very beautiful and effective character, displaying an abundance of native foliage, which is a slight departure

OPPOSITE: Vases of lilies, chrysanthemums and possibly daisies adorn the altar of St Thomas's Anglican Church, Newtown, Wellington, for Easter 1898. Lilies also feature on the altar cloth design. Missing, though, are the spring flowers so much a part of the festival in the northern hemisphere. C-5631-1/2, MCINTOSH ALBUM, ALEXANDER TURNBULL LIBRARY, WELLINGTON.

Father Francois Melu and altar boys at St Mary's Catholic Church, heart of the Marist mission at Pukekaraka, Otaki, at Easter 1884. Ferns feature among the decorations, and the traditional Easter Day text appears in both Maori and English above the altar. MARIST ARCHIVES, WELLINGTON.

Autumn harvest decorations, probably at St James's Anglican Church, Roxburgh, about 1895. Some Anglican churches used such fruits, vegetables and grains in their Easter decorations. Giant pumpkins, like the ones shown here, were a common feature of harvest festivals. S06-518D, HOCKEN COLLECTIONS, UARE TAOKA O HAKENA, UNIVERSITY OF OTAGO.

from former years, and renders the embellishments somewhat more in keeping with the Church of New Zealand. Ferns, flowers, and native shrubs are plentifully used throughout, and with great effect.'[72] As at Christmas, this use of native flora for Easter decorations demonstrated the adoption of indigenous items into Pakeha custom in line with Gibbons's model of 'cultural colonisation'.[73]

Another alternative to going native with Easter decorations was to stress the autumnal elements of the festival. As well as flowers and greenery, the decorations for Easter 1876 at St John's Anglican Church, Christchurch, included the scarlet berries so longed for by many migrants at Christmas.[74] Other congregations went further. A Pukekohe newspaper correspondent, attending the Easter service at St Andrew's Anglican Church in 1890, was 'taken by surprise to see the display of flowers, fruit, maize, wheat, barley, oats, and vegetables of several descriptions, and which were very tastefully arranged, showing what willing and loving hands can do to make God's house attractive'.[75] This Pukekohe service remained an Easter celebration, with sermon and hymns appropriate to the day, but a few New Zealand Anglican congregations spurned European tradition and incorporated their celebration of the harvest into the Easter festival. On Easter Day 1880 the altar of Nelson's Christ Church, later the Anglican Cathedral, displayed 'choice flowers relieved by baskets of fruit' for the 'special harvest thanksgiving services'.[76]

Church harvest festivals had a huge increase in popularity in late nineteenth-century New Zealand, as they did in Britain. All the Protestant churches, including those who continued to resist the celebration of Christmas and Easter, adopted this new service. By the turn of the century, Presbyterians and Baptists were decorating their churches with as many giant pumpkins and dangling carrots as their Anglican neighbours. Not all Anglican vicars approved of the innovation, which did not fit easily into their church calendar. Most kept it separate from Lent and Easter by holding it after the holy season had passed, commonly on 'Low Sunday', the first Sunday after Easter – they did not want this new tradition to eclipse the commemoration of the year's pivotal Christian festival.[77] Here they missed an opportunity to fit Easter more closely into the local environment. Perhaps this is not surprising, for the symbolism of Easter – death followed by new life – links much more naturally with spring than with autumn. Yet, those with a little imagination could demonstrate the events of Easter with seasonal products, like the grape vines and sheaves of wheat, symbols of the wine and bread of the last supper, used at St Patrick's Catholic Cathedral, Auckland, to decorate the altar of repose in 1890.[78] But in most churches the commemoration of Jesus' death and resurrection, and the celebration of God's provision of the harvest, remained separate events.

As well as flowers, greenery and in some cases grains, fruits and vegetables, on Easter Day churches displayed their finest furnishings and linen. This was the favoured time for making gifts to the church, and the congregation had the opportunity to enjoy for the first time donations which could range from handmade needlework to the finest silver communion ware. Easter Day 1890 saw the dedication of a 'very handsome' new side altar at St Mary's Catholic Church, Nelson. It had been created and donated by one of the parishioners, Mr R. Stewart.[79] In 1895 St Paul's Anglican Cathedral in Dunedin did particularly well with Easter gifts, receiving a gold chalice and paten (the vessels

The altar of the old Lutheran Church at Upper Moutere. Anna Heine, daughter of the pastor, noted in her diary that the altar cloth, bought with money she raised from the women of the congregation, was an Easter gift to the church in 1874. The picture of Jesus with a crown of thorns was an Easter 1875 addition. G-32547-1/2, C. M. HEINE COLLECTION, ALEXANDER TURNBULL LIBRARY, WELLINGTON.

used to present the communion wine and bread), silk burse (for storing the cover for the communion elements) and veil, Litany desk, sanctuary carpet, altar hanging, cruets (for storing communion wine) and hymn notice boards, as well as some generous donations of money.[80] Easter may have been a festival of Christian sacrifice; ironically, it also became the occasion for a display of the church's wealth.

The altar cloth and painting at the Upper Moutere Lutheran Church were both presented as Easter gifts during the 1870s. In this case the women of the congregation did not make the altar cloth themselves but instead raised the money for its purchase.[81] Women commonly took a special interest in the furnishing of their churches, making or donating many of the needlework items and providing most of the design and labour for the seasonal decorations. Leigh Schmidt, who has explored church decoration in the United States, suggests festive decorations were primarily devotional, aiming to glorify God and edify Christians. But they had other effects, not always as high-minded – for example, they could create competition between churches, and designers could become slaves to the latest fashion.[82] Church decorations were a source of prestige for their creators, generally women, who in some other respects played distinctly subordinate roles in the churches. Here was a great opportunity for women to play an active role in the celebration of church festivals by controlling the setting and demonstrating their horticultural and artistic skills.

The clergy as well as the church could be adorned. In 1897 the women of St Andrew's Anglican Church in Epsom, Auckland, presented their vicar, Eugene Gillam, with an Easter gift of 'a surplice of fine linen, a black silk stole, and a literate's hood'.[83] He also received £27 2s 4d from the combined Epsom and Ellerslie parish, which followed the Anglican tradition of giving all the Easter offerings directly to the vicar rather than adding them to the general church funds. In contrast with the other weeks of the year, churchwardens did not record the total of the offerings on Easter Day in their vestry books, considering this a private matter for the receiving clergyman. Sometimes, when the total was a generous one, it was made public. The system worked like a bonus, giving the best rewards to the most successful or most popular vicars, such as William Whyte of Picton and Koromiko whose 1885 parishioners 'testified their appreciation of the Rev Mr Whyte's ministry by contributing to the Easter Offertories a total of £34 8s 6d'.[84]

Needlework skills were also in evidence outside the churches, for wearing new clothes at Easter was an old custom. There is little evidence, though, to suggest that nineteenth-century New Zealanders wore festive new clothes to church at Easter: if they did, it created no public comment. In the northern hemisphere, Easter was the time when women first displayed their new spring finery, particularly new hats (sometimes nicknamed Easter bonnets). In late nineteenth-century New York, the people wandering between churches to see their floral displays evolved into the 'Easter parade', a show of the latest spring fashions.[85] The northern association between Easter and new spring clothes could not of course carry over to New Zealand, but it was possible for a link to develop between the festival and new autumn or winter finery. Clothing stores frequently advertised the arrival of the latest new season's fashions, but

Easter bonnets became popular in the early twentieth century, judging by some of the gorgeous hats on display at this Easter Carnival at Newtown Park, Wellington, in 1913. 'Aunt Sally' was a common attraction at sports days and larger picnics – the object of this throwing game was to hit the nose (or sometimes a pipe stuck in the mouth) of the figure of an old woman. G-47645-1/2, S. C. SMITH COLLECTION, ALEXANDER TURNBULL LIBRARY, WELLINGTON.

they were slow to connect these with Easter (unlike Christmas and New Year, which often received a mention in December and January advertisements for clothing). It may have been the growing significance of the Easter millinery tradition abroad (particularly in the United States) which alerted early twentieth-century New Zealand firms to the advantages of linking their products with the festival. In March 1910 Mrs Mathewson of Wellington advertised: 'Easter millinery! Just opened, for the Easter trade. A shipment of new millinery!' Mrs Mathewson's hats were not, however, the frivolous straw and floral confections of the northern Easter trade, but something altogether more practical for autumn: 'A very smart lot of Ready-to-Wears in Tweed and Felt, all good colours, at Reasonable Prices'.[86]

Another very old Easter tradition for which there is little evidence in nineteenth-century New Zealand is the Easter egg. The egg is an obvious symbol of fertility, and its association with ideas of rebirth and resurrection long predates Christianity. Besides its symbolism, the egg was linked with Easter because, in medieval times, it was forbidden during Lent – Easter Day was an opportunity to feast again on this and other luxury foods. In many parts of Europe people decorated their eggs, usually by colouring them, and the practice became popular in the north of England in the late eighteenth century. Decorated eggs became popular Easter gifts for children and in some districts various games involving the eggs – such as rolling them down hills – developed. Artificial eggs later grew in popularity. The very wealthy had coveted the fabulous bejewelled creations of master craftspeople from medieval times on, but simple confectionery eggs did not become common until the Victorian and Edwardian eras. Chocolate eggs first developed in France and Germany during the early nineteenth century, but it was not until late in the century that improved technology made the mass manufacture of the chocolate Easter egg possible. The delivery of Easter eggs by the Easter bunny came to Britain, like the Christmas tree and Santa Claus, from continental Europe via the United States, but not until the twentieth century. Like the egg, the rabbit is an old symbol of fertility, appropriate for a spring festival. In Germany, around the 1500s, the Easter hare (which later evolved into the Easter rabbit in English-speaking countries) became the bringer of Easter eggs.[87]

In 1894 the *New Zealand Herald* described the Easter egg as 'now a thing of the past'.[88] Perhaps there were not enough enthusiastic Easter egg eaters migrating to New Zealand to encourage a lively egg tradition in the colonial community. The practice received very little mention in contemporary sources, and the complete lack of advertising suggests that nineteenth-century Easter eggs were home-made. Local Catholic newspaper the *Tablet* did its bit to promote the custom in 1897 with the charming legend associating Easter eggs with a bird nesting in a tree over Jesus' tomb – the bird sang with joy when the stone was rolled away to reveal the empty tomb, and the angel blessed it with coloured eggs. 'So when you colour your Easter eggs think of the mother-bird that mourned for our dear Lord that first Easter morning, and that changed her song to a triumphant strain when the white robes of the angel shone

Two popular aspects of Easter in the northern hemisphere – Easter eggs and Easter bonnets – feature in this early twentieth-century Easter postcard, made by the Philco Publishing Co., London. Although never as popular as Christmas and New Year cards, Easter cards became part of the postcard craze of the early 1900s. This example was sent to Emily Coram of Waipiata by her sister Kate in Dunedin. FROM THE AUTHOR'S COLLECTION.

through the darkness, bringing light and joy to the world.'[89] The widespread popularity of Easter eggs in New Zealand dates from the early twentieth century, when modern chocolate melting and moulding techniques enabled local confectionery firms to make and market the hollow chocolate egg.

Today's other iconic Easter food – the hot cross bun – has quite a different history, for it was common in nineteenth-century New Zealand, though the buns may have been hard to come by in earlier years of European settlement before the establishment of numerous commercial bakeries. At Easter 1851 Vicesimus Lush, newly arrived as the Anglican vicar of Howick, wrote sadly in his diary that this was 'the first Good Friday I have ever past [sic] without *hot cross buns*'.[90] By the 1880s, though, hot cross buns were available at bakeries from the far north to the far south, from Mr Robinson's Excelsior Bakery in Whangarei to Crawford Brothers in Invercargill, which could supply 'Hot X Buns, in any quantities'.[91] Of course many New Zealanders made their own buns, just as they made their own bread. Jean Boswell, who grew up in a large family on newly cleared bush in rural Northland in the 1890s, recalled that her mother occasionally made currant buns as a special treat. Even better, at Easter she always made hot cross buns,

> minus the currants in the early days, but at least sweetened and marked with a cross. It wouldn't have been Easter otherwise. Easter buns were a special mixing, whether it was baking day or not, and they were always baked hot for breakfast. Oh, tide of home-sickness – rushing in on memory's strand of an Easter morning with the light flickering restlessly through the wind-stirred leaves, the scent of wattle blossoms, the smell of new milk and hot spicy buns![92]

Most people enjoyed their hot cross buns as a freshly-baked Good Friday breakfast treat. They could sometimes be bought on Thursday as well as Friday: in 1898 Dallen's of Queen Street, Auckland, advertised that 'for the convenience of our Country Customers we shall have a large Supply ready on Thursday, after 1 p.m.'.[93] Most town dwellers ordered their buns to be delivered on Good Friday morning. In 1890, at Napier, some people found the smell of the hot, spicy buns too tempting. Prowling the streets early on Good Friday, 'they watched the bakers' assistants delivering buns at houses ("delivering" meaning placing in a supposed secure place at the back of the house), and then went in and stole the articles'.[94]

Not everybody approved of hot cross buns. John Hobbs, the Anglican vicar at Naseby, declared in an 1880 sermon that the practice of eating hot cross buns was a 'most horrible one . . . it was an insult to Almighty God'.[95] Perhaps Hobbs had scruples about the superstitions surrounding the buns. Tradition had it that bread baked on Good Friday was particularly lucky, that it would not go stale and that it could be used as a cure for various ailments. Such belief in lucky days for baking no doubt predated Christian times, as did bread and cakes marked with a cross to honour various gods and goddesses. For Christians, the cross was the ultimate symbol of Jesus, and bread marked with a cross mimicked the host marked with a cross which was used for communion. Good Friday marked Jesus' crucifixion and on that day the communion host received special veneration; clearly it was the appropriate day to eat bread marked with a cross.[96]

How many New Zealanders believed in the lucky or curative powers of hot cross buns we cannot tell. The buns were certainly popular, but that was no doubt due to their delicious taste as much as belief in their supernatural power. Those who had been abstaining from luxury foods for the past six weeks found them particularly appealing. They were highly appreciated as a rare treat, served on just one day of the year, evocative of the season and of past times – like other holiday foods, hot cross buns have a strong flavour of nostalgia about them. The *New Zealand Herald*, describing in 1877 the 'ancient superstition' that bread baked on Good Friday had special curative properties, commented that 'the superstition is forgotten, while the custom, so far as the vending of the buns is concerned, is kept sacred'. Anyway, some bakers no longer made the buns on the lucky day: 'The Knights of the Dough, anxious for rest like other people, have so far departed from custom as to bake the buns on the day previous to Good Friday'.[97]

＊

At Easter 1898, as well as advertising hot cross buns, Auckland baker W. Parkinson of Victoria Street drew 'special attention to his new Picnic Luncheon Baskets, 1s and 2s Each, Containing Ham Sandwiches, Fruit Pies, &c. (Baskets Included)'.[98] This was a well-timed pitch, because Easter Monday was a popular day for outdoor recreation and picnics. 'Easter Monday is the second carnival of the year', declared an Auckland newspaper in 1881. 'It is the close of the summer and the precursor of the winter season.' Only New Year's Day was more popular for outings.[99]

In England, Easter Monday had a very long history as a day of sport and recreation. It was the remnant of a once longer Easter break that included Holy Week, a time for solemnity and contemplation, and the week after Easter, a time to indulge in the feasting, celebration and sports which had been forbidden during Lent. Following the Reformation, the authorities gradually whittled these holidays away until, by the early nineteenth century, only Good Friday, Easter Monday and Easter Tuesday remained, and by the end of the nineteenth century Easter Tuesday had also gone.[100] In early nineteenth-century Ireland, Easter Monday was a popular holiday, a mixture of religious observance and festive market day. But this mixture of religious and riotous activities disturbed the local bishops, and at their request the Pope proclaimed in 1829 that it was no longer a 'holiday of obligation' (a day when all Catholics should attend mass and abstain from work).[101] Most Scots ignored the holiday, as they did the rest of Easter.

In New Zealand, Easter Monday remained a popular holiday for the English and quickly spread to the whole community in most towns. In 1852 the fledgling community of Christchurch spent Easter Monday in good English fashion with a race meeting followed by a ball. The ball took place in the only available large room, a carpenter's shop, and was a great success, with dancing kept up until five in the morning. 'Everyone looked well, and wore a clean, if not a pretty, dress', reported Charlotte Godley.[102] Meanwhile, the Anglican children of Wellington enjoyed Easter Monday tea and cake at the government grounds with no less than Governor and Lady Grey. Their young Wesleyan friends had to content themselves with the schoolroom as a venue for their Sunday-school anniversary party on the same day. The Anglican and Methodist Sunday-school treats remained Easter Monday fixtures in Wellington for some years.[103]

Boat excursions to the North Shore proved a popular Easter Monday activity in Auckland, as did sports, like the quoits and foot races arranged by the proprietor of the Red Lion Inn in Drake Street for Easter Monday 1867. In 1882 some enterprising souls combined a visit to the North Shore, sports and Englishness by holding 'Ye Olde Englishe Fayre' at Takapuna – a crowd of 3000 enjoyed the athletics, bands and other entertainment, including a puppet show.[104] Dunedin, too, had a variety of Easter Monday excursions and entertainments on offer. Top marks for ingenuity go to the Volunteer Fire Brigade annual fête, which in 1866 attracted a large crowd to a day of Roman sports organised by James Cooke and the Great World Circus Company. The events, held in a 'grand hippodrome' at the North Dunedin Recreation Ground, included 'Roman races, chariot races, steeple-chases, flat races, and all the sports of the ancient Romans'.[105]

The holiday had less impact in rural areas, and many farmers probably ignored it altogether. Some small country towns did make something of Easter Monday by holding their annual races or sports. The 1871 Kaiapoi Athletic Sports were a great success – the most lively events involved chasing animals. One of the creatures in the sheep hunt ('prize the sheep') amused onlookers by escaping its pursuers through a hole in the fence. The haka display and hangi attracted an impressive crowd of 500 to the 1899 Wesleyan choir picnic and sports in the small rural Manawatu town of

A crowded paddle steamer heads up the Whanganui River on an excursion, Easter 1895. Easter Monday was one of the year's great days for indulging in outdoor recreation, as was Good Friday, for those without religious scruples. FROM THE AUTHOR'S COLLECTION.

Rongotea.[106] Country race days always attracted good crowds. The annual Easter Monday races in the small Otago town of Beaumont drew people from a wide surrounding district, not all of them great followers of the turf. As a reporter from nearby Lawrence commented, 'a great many residents, who care very little for racing, take their families out and meet friends from further up country, and make a kind of picnic of it'.[107]

Many Irish migrants happily adopted the holiday which had once been kept by their parents and grandparents. In some districts Hibernian societies, branches of the Catholic Friendly Society, held their annual sports on Easter Monday. The Oamaru Hibernian Society, founded in 1895, soon established the main annual Easter Monday event in their town. In 1899 they 'offered the public a really excellent afternoon's sports', attracting some of the best runners in the country. For those of a less serious bent,

'Excursionists – the early morning train' at Easter 1881. 'Our sketch depicts a characteristic scene always occurring just prior to the departure of a train on the occasion of holidays.' The excursionists include several hunters and a cricketer. *ILLUSTRATED NEW ZEALAND HERALD*, 16 JUNE 1881, P. 4.

'Mr Tyrell Turtil amused everyone with the uses to which he put his "bike" in some clever trick riding'.[108] Gore was another small town where Hibernian sports became the main feature of Easter Monday, attracting over a thousand holidaymakers in 1897.[109]

Easter Monday proved an ideal date for one of the more popular outdoor activities in nineteenth-century New Zealand (at least for men and boys): shooting. Those who did not have to work on Saturday and were thus fortunate enough to have four consecutive days of holiday could enjoy an extended hunting or fishing trip. In 1890 Nelson followers of the rod and rifle could take advantage of the *Lady Barkly*'s special excursion late on the Thursday before Easter to travel to French Pass, D'Urville Island and Pelorus Sound for a long weekend of sport.[110] Others travelled by railway, like the several men

A group of young men proudly display the bounty of a shooting expedition, Easter 1896.
Photographed at Waikumete Station, West Auckland. CI0815, AUCKLAND WAR MEMORIAL MUSEUM LIBRARY.

with guns pictured in the *Illustrated New Zealand Herald*'s 'characteristic scene' of Easter
excursionists in 1881. The Catlins district, on the South Otago coast, became a drawcard
for Easter hunters. In 1879 the place was 'alive with visitors. Included among them are
many Dunedinites spending the Easter holidays among our game'.[111]

It is difficult for us now to appreciate what hunting meant to nineteenth-century
migrants. Britain's hated game laws severely restricted access to hunting and fishing,
making them sports for gentlemen only. Hungry labourers tempted into poaching
risked severe consequences if caught. In New Zealand, anyone could hunt or fish:
although there were game laws, they were not much enforced, and licences were
cheap enough that all but the poorest could afford to shoot or fish legally.[112] Working-

class migrants revelled in this freedom to indulge in a once-forbidden activity, which became a potent symbol of release from the class strictures of Britain. Letters to family and friends in Britain abound with descriptions of the availability of game in their new country (almost all of it, aptly, also introduced from Britain). Joseph Brocklesby, a farm labourer from Lincolnshire now working near Hamilton, wrote home just a few months after his 1874 arrival in the colony. 'There are scores of pheasants, and you can go and shoot one when you think well, and no-one to interfere', he boasted.[113] John Gregory of Wellington had a similar tale. In addition to the pigs, rabbits, pigeons, ducks and goats, all readily available in the nearby bush, there were 'plenty of wild bulls, it is the best of beef; there is no one to say they are mine; those that get them have them'.[114]

•~

Many young men spent Easter taking part in another form of shooting: military training. Volunteers, the predecessors of today's Territorial Forces, had their origins in voluntary self-defence associations formed as early as the 1830s. Volunteer corps, generally with a strength of 50 to 100 men, eventually formed throughout the country, and some saw active service in the New Zealand Wars. In the mid-1880s, this part-time military force numbered 8000 or so, about one in 20 New Zealand men aged between 15 and 49. A few Maori participated alongside Pakeha, with some distinctively Maori corps, such as the Thames Native Rifle Volunteers (formed in 1874). Volunteer numbers declined from the late 1880s, but the force became popular again during the South African War.

Military experts were critical of the Volunteer system: the corps were too small for effective warfare; the officers (elected by their corps) had inadequate military knowledge; funding was insufficient to maintain effective arms and equipment; and the men lacked expert training. Some corps seemed more concerned with military pageantry, smart uniforms and fine bands than with the practicalities of preparing for warfare; they were as much social clubs as serious military forces. But until they were replaced with the new Territorial Force system in 1910, Volunteers were a popular and visible feature of the New Zealand landscape. The small corps had strong ties with local communities and the community took a great interest in their activities.[115]

Members of the Dunedin Artillery Volunteers (B Battery) photographed around the 1890s. Smart uniforms such as these were a feature of nineteenth-century volunteering and added to the spectacle of military parades and 'sham fights'. C/NEG E5289/29, HOCKEN COLLECTIONS, UARE TAOKA O HAKENA, UNIVERSITY OF OTAGO.

Volunteers gathered from many districts for their Easter camps or 'demonstrations', and the total numbers attending could be impressive. Locations changed from year to year, but often there were three or four events scattered through the country. In 1881, for example, there were Easter camps at Oamaru, Nelson and Te Awamutu, while in 1892 Volunteers gathered at Wanganui, Christchurch and Bluff. The camps usually followed a similar pattern. Those from out of town would arrive by train on Thursday evening or Friday morning and set up camp. They spent Thursday and Friday in various drills, Sunday was devoted to church parade and on Monday the gathering came to a climax with the 'sham fight' or major field exercise.[116] Smaller encampments could not always manage large field exercises. The 'demonstration' at Queenstown at Easter 1877 involved 230 Volunteers from this sparsely populated district. They were 'a

Etching of an early Volunteer Easter camp at Hillsborough, Christchurch, in 1865. About 3000 members of the public enjoyed the spectacle of the military parade. PHOTOCD4 IMG0065, AOTEAROA NEW ZEALAND CENTRE, CHRISTCHURCH CITY LIBRARIES.

splendid body of men' who managed to impress the locals: 'The novelty of the scene has caused quite an agreeable feeling in the town', reported a local correspondent. As well as the usual parades, drills and church services, this camp included a ball, band concert, shooting contest ('prize firing' in the language of the time) and regatta.[117] Not everyone had so much fun at their Easter exercises. In 1895 the Volunteer camp at Feilding ended up under two feet of water, while further south at Taiaroa Head, on the Otago Peninsula, bad weather made for miserable conditions for the Volunteers under canvas.[118]

For those who enjoyed the sight of men in uniform, the Volunteers' Easter exercises offered wonderful opportunities. William Brooks described the scene in Christchurch's Latimer Square at Easter 1880, as the Volunteers divided up and marched to the local churches for Easter Sunday services. 'A very grand sight for Christchurch seeing them marching to the various churches with a band leading each lot to the churches of each companies [sic] denomination. The denominational companies being asked to fall out . . . for instance, word of command from Major Lea, Presbyterians fall back,

The mock battles held at the Volunteers' Easter camps could attract many onlookers, as at this exercise staged in 1884 at Island Bay, Wellington. F-44040-1/2, ALEXANDER TURNBULL LIBRARY, WELLINGTON.

Roman Catholics march forward, Church of England stand at ease, thus they were at once selected.'[119] Large camps in rural districts often held outdoor services rather than attending local churches. In 1881, Catholics among the Volunteers in camp at Te Awamutu attended an Easter mass celebrated at the 'beautiful portable altar' of Father Augustine Luck, the local parish priest, a Benedictine who had recently arrived from England. This Te Awamutu camp was an impressive affair all round, with about 1100 Volunteers gathered from Auckland, Thames and Waikato. The Volunteers were outnumbered by the spectators though – two or three thousand people watched the demonstration and sham fight from the sidelines, some having arrived on the special trains put on just for camp spectators. The camp was not all hard work and military manoeuvres, for there was also an impressive amount of merrymaking, the nearby hotels doing a roaring trade in the evenings.[120] This may have been military training, but it was also a fine way to spend a holiday.

Volunteer camps were not all parades and military exercises – they also allowed opportunities for men to relax and enjoy one another's company. Here the No. 1 Waikato Mounted Rifles gather for an outdoor breakfast at the 1899 Easter encampment at Potter's Paddock, Epsom, Auckland. *AUCKLAND WEEKLY NEWS*, 14 APRIL 1899, SUPPLEMENT, P. 6. 7-AI7009, SPECIAL COLLECTIONS, AUCKLAND CITY LIBRARIES.

By the turn of the century, in most parts of New Zealand Good Friday had become a well-established holiday, though some residents continued to ignore it, particularly rural people from Scottish backgrounds. But Good Friday developed a different focus in the colony from that familiar to migrants from England, Ireland and continental Europe. While some New Zealanders kept the day as one of great religious significance, the most solemn in the year, they had to live in a community where many saw it as just another holiday, a day to enjoy a little rest and recreation. This does not mean New Zealand was less religious or more secular than other places. It indicates, rather, that the colony included people from a wide range of religious backgrounds, with different approaches to Easter. Anglicans may have been the largest denomination in the country, but they still made up less than half the population, and a strong and widespread belief in freedom of religion meant that no single church would ever be able to impose its ideas fully on New Zealand society as a whole.

Good Friday became a more religious holiday in the first few decades of the twentieth century, as New Zealand Presbyterians, Baptists and Congregationalists began to recognise the merits of keeping the Christian year. This was not simply because of their exposure to Anglican and Catholic ideas in their mixed colonial communities, although that perhaps helped. It reflected an international trend, as Protestant churches throughout the world developed a new appreciation of ritual. Until then, New Zealand Catholics and Anglicans faced the difficulties of keeping Lent and Holy Week while surrounded by temptations offered by those who had no appreciation for their customs. Anglicans in particular seem to have become far less diligent about Lent in the colonial environment, by the evidence of their clergy, at least.

Easter Monday presented fewer problems, although it was certainly not the best-kept holiday of the nineteenth century. This reflects, in part, its lack of commemorative purpose. It was a holiday for recreation, pure and simple, and because that meant, in the nineteenth century, a day spent outdoors, bad weather could destroy all its pleasure. At Dunedin in 1873 the holiday 'was almost a total failure, a large number of people attending to their avocations as usual. No doubt if the day had been fine many would have turned to pleasure instead of to business, but the wretched weather put outdoor enjoyment out of the question.'[121] And there were always some people reluctant to close down for what seemed a rather frivolous holiday. Many colonial business people would rather stay open and turn a profit than close for the day.

Autumn was as good a time as spring for an outdoor holiday, and Easter Monday sat as comfortably in the southern hemisphere as it did in the north. Some of the other traditions of Easter did not migrate so readily to the colony. Symbols of new life were ill-fitted to the autumn season, but New Zealanders were too closely attached to their northern roots to make any serious attempt to create new and more locally appropriate customs for the festival. Still, Easter has obviously survived as a major feature of the New Zealand holiday calendar. As more workers began to enjoy a five- rather than six-day working week, Easter became a much-appreciated extended break instead of two separate days off with work on the Saturday in between. It provided the last real chance for a holiday outing before the long nights of winter set in, and an ideal opportunity for a hunting trip or military camp. As Easter drew to a close, working

Lydia Williams and friends (possibly members of the Colledge family) camping at Poraiti, near Napier, during Easter 1888. For some, Easter allowed a long weekend break away from home. PHOTOGRAPH BY WILLIAM WILLIAMS, G-25637-1/1, E. R. WILLIAMS COLLECTION, ALEXANDER TURNBULL LIBRARY, WELLINGTON.

New Zealanders settled back into the drudgery of everyday life. They had just one red-letter day to look forward to (Queen Victoria's Birthday on 24 May) until late spring. Then the 'picnic season' would begin again with Labour Day (the second Wednesday in October) and the Prince of Wales's Birthday (9 November). Earlier generations had no holidays from May until December: for them everyday existence would continue until the next holiday season, Christmas, rolled around again.

The Evolution of the New Zealand Holiday

In early January 1872 the *Otago Witness* reflected on the holiday season just completed. The New Year had been welcomed 'with appropriate festive joy and temperate feasting'. The Englishman had 'distinguished the season . . . with the fair fat goose and a tankard of foaming ale' and the Scotsman 'by displaying in a gush of neighbourly hospitality his decided predilection for shortbread and whisky'. There was no reason to forget the 'old customs associated with the season . . . They are hallowed in our memories . . . we remember them all, and would not by forgetting them sever one link that in an innocent way attaches the past to the future'. The reverse of the seasons gave 'an advantage over the old country, for though the old associations with King Frost, the mistletoe bough, the long nights, and the cheerful fire, are thus partially destroyed, the summer days, instead of the dreary winter ones, afford an excellent opportunity for engaging in every description of out-door recreation'.[1]

Not everybody approved. 'Some churlish people are always complaining that we have too many holidays in the colonies – that they are a perfect bore', noted the Dunedin paper.[2] While some favoured business over leisure, others approved of holidays but found their timing inappropriate. In January 1886 a Maniototo correspondent expressed gratitude that the holidays were nearly past:

> We are antipodean in all things but we need not be in the matter of holidays. We could defer holding the Christmas Carnival until midwinter, and enjoy the orthodox 'plum duff' and other good cheer without any danger of indigestion waiting on appetite. This is worth a passing thought. In most places in Otago we have enforced holidays in winter, and the present system brings terrible disorganisation and loss of time.[3]

Such pleas had little effect. Summer holidays may have been inconvenient for farmers, but most other workers greatly appreciated their Christmas and New Year breaks, and the opportunity they gave for outdoor enjoyment at the warmest time of year.

Outdoor recreation was the central feature of holidays in New Zealand and, in the case of Christmas and New Year, this made them distinctly different from the holidays of the northern hemisphere. New Zealanders loved picnics and excursions and being in the bush or at the seaside. Some of those fortunate enough to have extended holiday breaks camped out, for the ultimate wilderness experience. Others simply visited a beauty spot within walking distance of their homes. At New Year 1887, during their courting days, Dunedin's Jack Fowler and Jeannie Broome enjoyed 'a picnic of two' at a nearby waterfall.[4] On Good Friday the following year, they went 'to Mount Allen which is some 18 mile up on the great talked of (here) Otago Central Railway . . . I took two of Jeannies sisters and Shepherd and Cole turned up and we lit a fire and boiled the tea in a billy and fairly enjoyed ourselves at a picnic'. But this was no intimate excursion, as Jack went on to explain: 'I thought half of Dunedin were there; there were two trains crowded the papers gave the number as 1500 a great number took guns with them and the bunnies got a scare'.[5]

This large railway excursion was typical of the holiday experiences of many nineteenth-century New Zealanders. Urban factory workers and rural families alike, they were, on the whole, sociable people, who enjoyed large community gatherings; even when exploring the wilderness they often spent their holidays among crowds. Sports, regattas, horse races and Caledonian games were also popular (and often crowded) ways of spending the holidays. They were community gatherings in the true sense of the word community, for they were occasions where Maori and Pakeha met and mingled, in an era when such meetings could be rare in some districts. Some sports meetings had segregated events, but in others Pakeha and Maori competed alongside one another, with Pakeha often bested by Maori sporting enthusiasm and skill. On Easter Monday 1876 at Waitara, the site of bitter warfare just sixteen years earlier, Maori proved their sporting prowess by winning events ranging from canoeing to climbing the greasy pole.[6]

Holidays brought communities together, but they were also an important time for families. Colonial families could be large and scattered over wide distances, but they made a special effort to get together at the times which meant the most to them: Christmas for the English and Irish and their descendants; New Year for the Scots.

Excursionists in the 1890s admire the view from a viaduct in the Rangiora district. Holiday excursions often involved crowds. C-26416-1/2, PACOLL-7581-74, ALEXANDER TURNBULL LIBRARY, WELLINGTON.

Those without families gathered instead with friends or colleagues to enjoy a little holiday cheer, like the goldminers, gumdiggers and shepherds who created their plum puddings in isolated and spartan conditions. Jack Fowler, who had migrated alone to New Zealand, spent his first colonial Christmas at his lodgings with other single men, their landlady providing a feast of poultry, a great sirloin of beef, two or three pies and the Christmas pudding sent by Jack's mother from England. Jack helped out with preparations by wringing the necks of the hen and ducks that were to grace their plates. The following year he also had Christmas dinner at his lodgings, then in the evening he 'went to the house of one of our old bo[a]rders who got married some time ago and seems to be getting on well'.[7] His old shipboard mates and former lodgers provided Jack Fowler with a surrogate family until he could establish a new one of his own. All the evidence about holidays (and there is plenty of it) suggests that family and community links were powerful and significant in nineteenth-century New Zealand. There is little here to support Miles Fairburn's controversial argument that colonial society was fragmented and 'atomised': even 'isolated' single men often celebrated the holidays with others.[8]

'Home for the holidays', the goal of many scattered New Zealand families. *ILLUSTRATED NEW ZEALAND HERALD*, 26 JANUARY 1883, P. 8.

Many New Zealanders revelled in their holidays. They wrote with pride of their frequency (in comparison with Britain), of the opportunities to visit the outdoors and of the land's abundance, symbolised especially in huge Christmas dinners and in hunting trips. But not everything about the holidays was rosy. Migrants missed their distant loved ones especially strongly on those occasions when families traditionally gathered. They also missed, often deeply, the holiday traditions which could not feature in their new setting: holly berries at Christmas; the cosy fire of a winter New Year's Eve; the spring flowers of Easter. They clung tenaciously to those northern-hemisphere traditions which could be retained in the southern hemisphere, no matter how inappropriate in the new environment. Sarah Derry, a Christchurch teacher visiting friends 'up country' in the midst of harvesting, wrote to her cousin in Nottingham at Christmas 1875: 'I expect it seems strange to you, nearly all Christmas Day we were sitting out in the fields it was so very hot it seems so ridiculous keeping up the fashion of plum pudding and roast beef when blancmange and cold joints are preferable'.[9] Although they knew such behaviour was incongruous, colonists and their descendants continued (and many New Zealanders still continue) the customs which formed a link they were not willing to break with their cultural heritage.

When necessary, nineteenth-century New Zealanders found substitutes for old holiday practices. New Year became a time for Caledonian games rather than indoor drinking sports. Settlers decorated their homes and churches with pohutukawa, rata and ripe cherries instead of holly berries at Christmas, and with chrysanthemums and newly harvested vegetables instead of spring flowers at Easter. Necessity became a virtue: many relished the use of native flora as they increasingly identified with the land they had come to love, or in which they had been born. Much as they had appropriated Maori land, Pakeha adopted indigenous flora and fauna into their own evolving culture. But Peter Gibbons's idea of cultural colonisation can only go so far in explaining the development of New Zealand's holidays.[10] Certainly the holidays were significant agents of colonisation, ways to make Pakeha feel they 'owned' and controlled the space they called New Zealand; ways, moreover, of making New Zealand feel like 'home'. But it is important also to acknowledge that Maori adopted and adapted these holidays and made them their own. We need to recognise too that migrants encountered and sometimes adopted unfamiliar holiday customs from European settlers of different regional and religious backgrounds. This mingling of different migrant customs, along with the necessary adaptations to southern-hemisphere conditions, was what made New Zealand holiday traditions most distinctive.

The holidays were more secular in New Zealand than in England or Ireland, and for that we can blame – or thank – the Scots. Compared to the distribution of population in the British Isles, the Scots were over-represented among nineteenth-century migrants to New Zealand, and that had a significant impact on culture and religion. The Scots brought with them their favourite holiday, New Year, plus a suspicion of the holidays taken for granted by other European migrants, Christmas and Easter. They adopted these holidays readily enough when living in mixed communities, but remained wary about their religious observance well into the twentieth century. This had an impact on the rest of the community. Anglicans, especially, found it challenging to maintain their Lent and Good Friday traditions in New Zealand.

But New Zealand was not an irreligious country: it was sectarianism rather than secularism which made the holidays less religious. The great majority of nineteenth-century New Zealanders held an allegiance to Christianity, and most of those who did not held other spiritual beliefs – they were Jews, Buddhists or followers of various Maori religious movements. Within Christianity, the range of denominations, none of them a majority, made for a varied and sometimes contested approach to religious practice, including the keeping of holidays.

Still, over 60 per cent of Pakeha and most Christian Maori belonged to the three churches which celebrated the festivals of the Christian year: enough that these holidays did retain a significant religious element in the colony. Many Anglicans, Catholics and Methodists attended special services for Christmas and Easter, decorating their churches for the occasion; they sang carols and admired nativity scenes at Christmas; and they mourned the death of Jesus on Good Friday and celebrated his resurrection on Easter Day. Their neighbours may have been attending picnics instead, but the religious tradition remained powerful. Methodists and Anglicans managed to reverse the downgrade of the spiritual side of the holidays by making New Year – the great secular holiday of the Scots – a more religious occasion, with their special watch night church services.

Christmas, New Year and Easter remain important holidays in twenty-first-century New Zealand. All New Zealand workers are now entitled to a minimum of three weeks of paid annual leave each year (shortly to increase to four weeks), a luxury undreamed of by their nineteenth-century forebears. But our public holiday calendar remains little different from that which evolved from the mixture of cultural and religious traditions of colonial New Zealand. The two holidays added more recently to the public holiday schedule are more indigenous than our older ones, but they are no longer new. Anzac Day has been a national holiday since 1920, and Waitangi Day since 1973 (having been a holiday in Northland prior to that). New Zealand has no public holidays for holidays' sake (the 'summer bank holiday' and 'spring bank holiday' of Britain) or holidays to celebrate modern heroes (Mahatma Gandhi in India, Martin Luther King in the United States): all of our holidays commemorate an historic event or tradition.

In the twenty-first century, festivals from non-European cultures, once marginalised in 'mainstream' New Zealand society, have become increasingly visible in the local

Chinese goldminers at Waikaia, Southland, around the turn of the century. Like these men, many nineteenth-century Chinese migrants lived on the goldfields, and the great majority were male. They celebrated their own festivals, but it was only with a new wave of Asian migration in the twentieth century that occasions like Chinese New Year became well known and popular with the wider community. PHOTOGRAPH BY GEORGE MCNEUR, S06-294-E2448/5, HOCKEN COLLECTIONS, UARE TAOKA O HAKENA, UNIVERSITY OF OTAGO.

landscape, though they show little sign of becoming formal public holidays here. However, they do receive support from local government. In recent years, for example, the Wellington and Auckland City Councils have promoted Diwali, the Hindu Festival of Lights, and the Auckland and Dunedin City Councils have sponsored the celebration of Chunjie, the Chinese New Year.[11] New Zealand shows little propensity to add or remove holidays, although some have suggested in recent years that it would be more appropriate to take a holiday for Matariki than for the 'official' birthday of the monarch in winter. Still we cling to old traditions: Elizabeth II has been our head of state for over 50 years, but we continue to recognise her with a holiday fixed at the date of the birthday of her grandfather, George V, who became King in 1910.

Our modern holiday practices still reflect the culture established in the nineteenth-century colonisation of Aotearoa. They are a lively mixture of old-world tradition and the new-world environment; of the religious and the secular; of the family and the broader community. They show the mixture of people who made up the colonial community; people with a diversity of cultural backgrounds too readily forgotten. Twenty-first-century New Zealanders celebrating Christmas, New Year and Easter may like to spare a thought for those who contributed towards our holiday traditions: Maori with their magnificent Christmas hakari; the English, who insisted on eating roast beef in midsummer but also enjoyed their strawberries and cream; Germans, who lit up their homes and churches with Christmas trees; Scots, who greeted the New Year with whisky and 'Auld Lang Syne'; and Irish Catholics, who married at Shrovetide and ate fish through Lent. All played a role in the development of that ever-evolving ritual, the New Zealand holiday.

ABBREVIATIONS

ATL	Alexander Turnbull Library, Wellington
HBH	*Hawkes Bay Herald*
HC	Hocken Collections, Dunedin
NZP	*N.Z. Presbyterian*
NEM	*Nelson Evening Mail*
NZH	*New Zealand Herald*
NZJH	*New Zealand Journal of History*
NZS	*New Zealand Spectator and Cook's Strait Guardian*
NZT	*New Zealand Tablet*
ODT	*Otago Daily Times*
OSM	Otago Settlers Museum, Dunedin
OW	*Otago Witness*
PWT	*Palmerston & Waikouaiti Times*
PCA	Presbyterian Church Archives, Dunedin
SC	*Southern Cross*
ST	*Southland Times*
TH	*Taranaki Herald*
DNZB	*The Dictionary of New Zealand Biography*
WT	*Waikato Times*
WH	*Wanganui Herald*
WI	*Wellington Independent*
WCT	*West Coast Times*

INTRODUCTION: SEASONAL CELEBRATIONS AND THE MAKING OF NEW ZEALAND CULTURE

1 Charles Hayward diary, 25 December 1865 and 1 January 1866, AB-023, OSM, Dunedin. For an explanation of 'first footing', see pp. 85–6.

2 Eviatar Zerubavel, *Hidden Rhythms: Schedules and Calendars in Social Life*, University of Chicago Press, Chicago, 1981, especially p. 70; Zerubavel, *The Seven Day Circle: The History and Meaning of the Week*, Free Press, New York, 1985. For a popular and reliable history of the calendar, see also E. G. Richards, *Mapping Time: The Calendar and its History*, Oxford University Press, New York, 1998.

3 K. S. Inglis, *The Australian Colonists: An Exploration of Social History 1788–1870*, Melbourne University Press, Carlton, 1974, pp. 65–152.

4 For discussion of these other holidays, see Alison Clarke, 'Feasts and Fasts: Holidays, Religion and Ethnicity in Nineteenth-Century Otago', PhD thesis, University of Otago, 2003; Clarke, '"With one accord rejoice on this glad day": Celebrating the Monarchy in Nineteenth-Century Otago', *NZJH* 36, 2 (2002), pp. 137–60; Clarke, '"Days of Heaven on Earth": Presbyterian Communion Seasons in Nineteenth-Century Otago', *Journal of Religious History* 26, 3 (2002), pp. 274–97; Bert Roth, 'Labour Day in New Zealand', in John E. Martin and Kerry Taylor, eds *Culture and the Labour*

Movement, Dunmore Press, Palmerston North, 1991, pp. 304–14.

5   An exception is Shirley Maddock and Michael Easther, *A Christmas Garland: A New Zealand Christmas Album 1642–1900 in Twelve Parts*, Collins, Auckland, 1980. Two influential historians have briefly explored the holidays of nineteenth-century New Zealand, only to dismiss them as failures. See Keith Sinclair, *A Destiny Apart: New Zealand's Search for National Identity*, Allen & Unwin, Wellington, 1986, pp. 177–87 (for Sinclair, all holidays were insignificant until Anzac Day, the true national day, arrived); Miles Fairburn, *The Ideal Society and its Enemies: The Foundation of Modern New Zealand Society 1850–1900*, Auckland University Press, Auckland, 1989, pp. 161–2; Fairburn, *Nearly out of Heart and Hope: The Puzzle of a Colonial Labourer's Diary*, Auckland University Press, Auckland, 1995, pp. 202–7 (for Fairburn, holidays supposedly failed to bring communities together, supporting his controversial thesis that colonial New Zealand was an atomised society). On Anzac Day, see Sinclair, *Destiny Apart*, pp. 82–4; Maureen Sharpe, 'Anzac Day in New Zealand 1916 to 1939', *NZJH* 15, 2 (1981), pp. 97–114; Stephen Clarke, '"The One Day of the Year": Anzac Day in Aotearoa/New Zealand 1946–1990', MA thesis, University of Otago, 1994; Scott Worthy, 'A Debt of Honour: New Zealanders' First Anzac Days', *NZJH* 36, 2 (2002), pp. 185–200.

6   For a useful review of the Christmas literature, see Neil Armstrong, 'Christmas in Nineteenth-Century Britain and America: A Historiographical Overview', *Cultural and Social History* 1 (2004), pp. 118–25. Major studies include Daniel Miller, ed., *Unwrapping Christmas*, Oxford University Press, Oxford, 1993; William B. Waits, *The Modern Christmas in America: A Cultural History of Gift Giving*, New York University Press, New York, 1993; Penne L. Restad, *Christmas in America: A History*, Oxford University Press, Oxford, 1995; Stephen Nissenbaum, *The Battle for Christmas*, Vintage, New York, 1996; Mark Connelly, *Christmas: A Social History*, Tauris, London, 1999; Karal Ann Marling, *Merry Christmas! Celebrating America's Greatest Holiday*, Harvard University Press, Cambridge, Massachusetts, 2000; J. M. Golby and A. W. Purdue, *The Making of the Modern Christmas*, rev.

edn, Sutton, Stroud, Gloucestershire, 2000. Easter and New Year have received less attention from historians, but feature in two major studies which also include important discussions of Christmas: see Leigh Eric Schmidt, *Consumer Rites: The Buying and Selling of American Holidays*, Princeton University Press, Princeton, 1995; Ronald Hutton, *The Stations of the Sun: A History of the Ritual Year in Britain*, Oxford University Press, Oxford, 1996.

7   James Belich, *Paradise Reforged: A History of the New Zealanders from the 1880s to the Year 2000*, Penguin, Auckland, 2001, p. 216.

8   Hutton, *Stations of the Sun*, pp. 1–8; Susan K. Roll, *Toward the Origins of Christmas*, Kok Pharos, Kampen, 1995; Joseph F. Kelly, *The Origins of Christmas*, Liturgical Press, Collegeville, Minnesota, 2004.

9   Hutton, *Stations of the Sun*, pp. 179–81.

10 Ian Pool, *Te Iwi Maori: A New Zealand Population Past, Present and Projected*, Auckland University Press, Auckland, 1991.

11 Figures calculated from the country of birth of those born outside New Zealand in the New Zealand census tables, 1858–1901. For a graphic display of the birthplace of colonists in 1874, see 'The Colony in 1874: Town, Country and Goldfield', in Malcolm McKinnon, ed., *New Zealand Historical Atlas*, Bateman, Auckland, 1997, plate 53.

12 Terry Hearn, 'The Origins of New Zealand's Irish Settlers, 1840–1945', in Brad Patterson, ed., *The Irish in New Zealand: Historical Contexts and Perspectives*, Stout Research Centre, Wellington, 2002, pp. 15–34.

13 Terry Hearn, 'English', in *Te Ara: The Encyclopedia of New Zealand*, updated 11 July 2005, www.TeAra. govt.nz/NewZealanders/NewZealandPeoples/English/en.

14 Rosalind McClean, 'Scottish Emigrants to New Zealand, 1840–1880: Motives, Means and Background', PhD thesis, University of Edinburgh, 1990, pp. 118, 436.

15 John Stenhouse, 'God's Own Silence: Secular Nationalism, Christianity and the Writing of New Zealand History', *NZJH* 38, 1 (2004), pp. 52–71.

16 Alison Clarke, '"Tinged with Christian Sentiment": Popular Religion and the Otago Colonists, 1850–1900', in John Stenhouse and G. A. Wood, eds, *Christianity, Modernity and Culture: New Perspectives*

on *New Zealand History*, ATF Press, Adelaide, 2005, pp. 103–31.

17 Figures from the New Zealand census – the 1901 census has a convenient summary table covering the period 1878–1901.

18 Allan Davidson, *Christianity in Aotearoa*, 3rd edn, Education for Ministry, Wellington, 2004, pp. 8–18, 43–8, 130–4.

19 Figures calculated from the New Zealand census tables. For a graphic display of religious allegiance at a slightly later date, 1921, see McKinnon, *New Zealand Historical Atlas*, plates 69 and 70.

20 Thomas Adam diaries, 1878–86, M-107, OSM. Herries Beattie recorded extracts from Adam's 1876–71 diaries, MS-0582-F/1, HC.

21 'Recollections of William Smaill from 1858 to 1862–3 around Mayfield Farm', p. 25, C-098, OSM.

22 Hugh Jackson, 'Churchgoing in Nineteenth-Century New Zealand', *NZJH* 17, 1 (1983), pp. 43–59. Methodists – the smaller English-dominated denomination – were the most diligent of all churchgoers; Catholics fell between Methodists and Presbyterians.

23 John Christie sermon, December 1892, DA12/1, 3/137, PCA; John Christie diary, 26 December 1888 and 29 April 1889, AG-102, OSM.

24 Hutton, *Stations of the Sun*, 1996, pp. 25–33, 196–7; F. Marian McNeill, *The Silver Bough, Volume Three: A Calendar of Scottish National Festivals, Hallowe'en to Yule*, Maclellan, Glasgow, 1961, pp. 58–61; Alexander Wright, *The Presbyterian Church: Its Worship, Functions, and Ministerial Orders*, Oliphant Anderson & Ferrier, Edinburgh, 1895, pp. 36–7; Margo Todd, 'Profane Pastimes and the Reformed Community: The Persistence of Popular Festivities in Early Modern Scotland', *Journal of British Studies* 39 (2000), pp. 123–56.

25 *Labourer* (Boston), 1 July 1876, p. 1, cited in Rollo Arnold, *The Farthest Promised Land: English Villages, New Zealand Immigrants of the 1870s*, Victoria University Press, Wellington, 1981, p. 155.

26 Clement A. Miles, *Christmas Customs and Traditions: Their History and Significance*, Dover, New York, 1976, p. 322 (first published as *Christmas in Ritual and Tradition, Christian and Pagan* in 1912).

27 Hutton, *Stations of the Sun*, p. 122. On the English adoption of New Year, initially influenced by Scottish migrants to the south, see also Miles, *Christmas Customs*, p. 327.

28 Kevin Danaher, *The Year in Ireland: Irish Calendar Customs*, Irish Books & Media, Minneapolis, 1972, pp. 258–62; Robert H. Buchanan, 'Calendar Customs: Part 1. New Year's Day to Michaelmas', *Ulster Folklife* 8 (1962), pp. 15–17; Philip Robinson, 'Harvest, Halloween, and Hogmanay: Acculturation in Some Calendar Customs of the Ulster Scots', in Jack Santino, ed., *Halloween and Other Festivals of Death and Life*, University of Tennessee Press, Knoxville, 1994, pp. 3–23.

29 *SC*, 1 February 1850, p. 2.

30 *SC*, 29 January 1850, p. 3.

31 Sinclair, *Destiny Apart*, p. 178.

32 The development of holiday legislation in both Britain and New Zealand is complex and there are few relevant studies – I have relied mostly on the statutes themselves. A brief but useful summary of the New Zealand situation (which does not include all of the early legislation) is the booklet *Workers' Holidays in New Zealand: A Brief History*, Trade Union History Project, Wellington, 1997. For Britain, see Alice Russell, *Bank Holidays: A Victorian Invention and Modern Institution*, Minerva, London, 2000.

33 *NZH*, 3 January 1878, p. 3.

34 John Wither to Margaret Wither, 14 January 1880, Misc-MS-1238, HC.

35 *NZH*, 4 January 1879, p. 6.

36 *OW*, 30 December 1865, p. 9.

37 *NZH*, 2 January 1868, p. 6; 30 March 1869, p. 3; 4 January 1870, p. 4; 6 April 1871, p. 5.

38 John George Walker, 'Letters home, chiefly from the Otago Goldfields, 1862–1863', MS-0296, HC.

39 *NZH*, 21 December 1885, p. 5.

40 *PWT*, 12 March 1880, p. 2. For other examples of harvest holidays in Otago schools, see *OW*, 11 February 1882, p. 13; 18 February 1882, p. 13; 4 March 1882, p. 13.

41 Kay Matthews, *Behind Every School: The History of the Hawke's Bay Education Board*, Hawke's Bay Education Board, Napier, 1988, p. 50.

42 Frederick Barkas, 'Some Memories of a Mediocrity', Volume 5, pp. 2–5, MS-Papers-2491-05, ATL.

43 Jack Fowler to Martha Fowler, 23 March 1891, Fowler letters, OSM.

44 Fowler letters.

1   'The Sailor's Journal', in Robert McNab, ed., *Historical Records of New Zealand, Vol II*, Government Printer, Wellington, 1914, p. 32. This translation of the journal of an unidentified sailor describes a feast on 25 November 1642, but a comparison with Tasman's journal shows that the month should be December.

2   J. C. Beaglehole, ed., *The Endeavour Journal of Joseph Banks, Vol I*, Angus & Robertson, Sydney, 1962, pp. 448–9.

3   John Dunmore, trans and ed., *The Expedition of the St Jean-Baptiste to the Pacific 1769–1770*, Hakluyt Society, London, 1981, pp. 228–91. On debates over the 'first' Christian service in New Zealand, see also John Dunmore, 'The First Christian Service: 1769, 1801 or 1814?', *Auckland–Waikato Historical Journal* 41 (1982), pp. 17–18.

4   Anne Salmond, *Between Worlds: Early Exchanges between Maori and Europeans 1773–1815*, Viking, Auckland, 1997, pp. 289–92.

5   Salmond, *Between Worlds*, pp. 436, 464–5. In 1957 Willow Macky immortalised the occasion in her popular hymn 'Te Harinui', one of the best-known local Christmas songs.

6   Lachlan Langlands, 'The First Christmas in Dunedin', BR File 20/17, OSM. Langlands had been present at the occasion. By the time Justice of the Peace David Garrick read the Riot Act and swore in special constables, the fighting had ended and no harm seems to have come to the township from this Christmas revelry. See also *Otago News*, 27 December 1848, p. 2.

7   Lawrence M. Rogers, ed., *The Early Journals of Henry Williams 1826–40*, Pegasus, Christchurch, 1961, p. 209.

8   Hutton, *Stations of the Sun*, pp. 95–123; see also Nissenbaum, *Battle for Christmas*, pp. 90–131.

9   J. W. Stack, *Early Maoriland Adventures*, ed. A. H. Reed, Oxford University Press, London, 1937, p. 42. Stack later became a missionary himself. 'Mr Brown' was Rev. Alfred Brown.

10 James Watkin diary, 28 December 1840, 27 December 1841, 26 December 1842, 26 December 1843, MS-0440/004, HC.

11 Anne Salmond, *Hui: A Study of Maori Ceremonial Gatherings*, Reed, Auckland, 2004, pp. 18, 107.

12 William Morley, *The History of Methodism in New Zealand*, McKee, Wellington, 1900, pp. 170–1.

13 *Maori Messenger/Te Karere Maori*, January 1860, p. 10.

14 *Te Waka Maori o Niu Tirani*, 25 January 1876, p. 12.

15 *NZH*, 30 December 1880, p. 6. On Kaihau, an important figure in the King Movement, later a Member of the House of Representatives, see 'Kaihau, Henare', in *DNZB*, Vol. Two, *1870–1900*, Bridget Williams / Department of Internal Affairs, Wellington, 1993, pp. 250–1.

16 On Christmas in Ireland, see Danaher, *Year in Ireland*, pp. 233–58; and Ronald H. Buchanan, 'Calendar Customs: Part 2. Harvest to Christmas', *Ulster Folklife* 9 (1963), pp. 71–3.

17 Jackson, 'Churchgoing in Nineteenth-Century New Zealand'.

18 Alison Drummond, ed., *The Auckland Journals of Vicesimus Lush 1850–63*, Pegasus, Christchurch, 1971, p. 97.

19 *NZH*, 31 December 1896, p. 6.

20 *NZH*, 3 January 1878, p. 3.

21 *NZH*, 28 December 1868, p. 5.

22 St Peter's Anglican Church, Caversham, Service Record Book, 1877–1884, AG-040/020, HC.

23 *PWT*, 29 December 1882, p. 2.

24 *NZH*, 28 December 1868, p. 5.

25 William Francis ('Frank') Barraud diary, 24 December 1871, MS-Papers-0089-01, ATL.

26 Alison Drummond, ed., *The Thames Journals of Vicesimus Lush 1868–82*, Pegasus, Christchurch, 1975, p. 185.

27 *NZT*, 3 January 1874, p. 7.

28 *NZT*, 4 January 1895, p. 17.

29 *OW*, 13 December 1879, p. 8.

30 Hugh Keyte and Andrew Parrott, eds, *The New Oxford Book of Carols*, Oxford University Press, Oxford, 1992; Ian Bradley, *Abide with Me: The World of Victorian Hymns*, SCM, London, 1997.

31 *OW*, 30 December 1876, p. 15.

32 Hutton, *Stations of the Sun*, p. 120.

33 *NZH*, 25 December 1883, p. 5.

34 Frank Barraud diary, 25 December 1870.

35 Peter F. Anson, *Fashions in Church Furnishings 1840–1940*, 2nd edn, Studio Vista, London, 1965; Jack Goody, *The Culture of Flowers*, Cambridge University Press, Cambridge, 1993, p. 303.

36 *NZH*, 26 December 1878, p. 2.

37 *NZT*, 1 January 1892, p. 18.

38 Hutton, *Stations of the Sun*, p. 426.

39 Charlotte Godley to Sarah Wynne, 30 January 1851, quoted in John R. Godley, ed., *Letters from Early New Zealand by Charlotte Godley 1850–1853*, Whitcombe & Tombs, Christchurch, 1951, p. 156.

40 Alison Drummond, ed., *The Waikato Journals of Vicesimus Lush 1864–8, 1881–2*, Pegasus, Christchurch, 1982, p. 43.

41 *NZH*, 28 December 1897, p. 3.

42 Peter Gibbons, 'Cultural Colonization and National Identity', *NZJH* 36, 1 (2002), pp. 5–17.

43 Virginia M. Perry, ed., *Eliza's Journal: A Gentlewoman's Experiences in New Zealand in the late 1850s*, the editor, Dunedin, 2004, p. 15.

44 Francis Redwood, *Reminiscences of Early Days in New Zealand*, C. M. Banks, Wellington, 1922, p. 14.

45 Memoirs of Emma Chisholm (née Allen), Allen family papers, MS-Papers-0441, Folder 5, ATL.

46 *NZH*, 26 December 1883, p. 5.

47 Drummond, *Thames Journals of Vicesimus Lush*, p. 45.

48 *NZH*, 28 December 1885, p. 4.

49 *NZT*, 1 January 1886, p. 16.

50 *NZT*, 31 December 1886, p. 16; 28 December 1888, p. 18; 2 January 1891, p. 5.

51 See Clarke, 'Feasts and Fasts', for details of the development of Christmas in Otago.

52 George Hepburn to Thomas Martin, 29 December 1858; George Hepburn to his sister, 20 January 1868; William Downie Stewart papers, MS-0985-035/002 and MS-0985-035/003, HC.

53 *OW*, 3 January 1857, p. 4.

54 *NZP*, 1 January 1898, p. 121.

55 *St Andrew's Church Monthly*, December 1885, p. 5, PCA; *OW*, 2 January 1886, p. 13.

56 For example, see *NZH*, 27 December 1879, p. 5.

57 Reported regularly in the press – see, for example, *NZH*, 28 December 1885, p. 4.

58 First Church Dunedin Session Minute Book, 7 December 1891, PCA.

59 *Proceedings of the General Assembly of the Presbyterian Church of New Zealand, 1932*, Otago Daily Times, Dunedin, 1932, pp. 12, 154.

60 *WI*, 26 December 1857, p. 3.

61 Ellen Smith (née Windsor), 'Not a Poor Thing: Random Memories 1888–1968', p. 13, MS-Papers-2397, ATL.

62 Drummond, *Thames Journals of Vicesimus Lush*, p. 185.

63 *NZH*, 26 December 1876, p. 2.

64 *Timaru Herald*, 26 December 1899, p. 2.

65 *NZH*, 26 December 1883, p. 5. Moody and Sankey were Victorian preachers and hymn writers.

66 *NZH*, 25 December 1877, p. 2.

67 *PWT*, 29 December 1882, p. 2.

68 *OW*, 29 December 1877, p. 15.

69 *NZH*, 27 December 1875, p. 2.

70 *OW*, 24 December 1881, p. 21.

71 *OW*, 22 December 1892, p. 25.

72 Samuel Stephens diary, 25 December 1853, MS-2055, ATL.

73 Jemima Martin to Mary Kempe, 16 August 1852, Jemima and Albin Martin correspondence, MS-Papers-2136/2, ATL.

74 Thomas Ferens to his sister and brother, March 1850, Thomas Ferens papers, Box 1, AG-99, OSM.

75 *NZH*, 3 January 1873, p. 4.

76 *OW*, 25 December 1858, p. 4.

77 *WCT*, 25 December 1867, p. 2.

78 Postal regulations published in the *New Zealand Gazette*, 7 July 1892, pp. 986–7.

79 Connelly, *Christmas*, p. 100.

80 Brenda Guthrie Northcroft, *New Zealand Memories*, 2nd edn, Reed, Wellington, 1959, p. 69.

81 Charlotte Godley to Sarah Wynne, 30 January 1851, in Godley, *Letters from Early New Zealand*, p. 155.

82 *NZS*, 28 December 1850, p. 2.

83 *WI*, 25 December 1862, p. 3.

84 *NZH*, 24 December 1872, p. 2.

85 *NZS*, 20 December 1851, p. 2.

86 *NZH*, 25 December 1888, p. 5.

87 *OW*, 9 January 1869, p. 5.

88 C. Anne Wilson, *Food and Drink in Britain*, Penguin, Harmondsworth, 1976, pp. 283–8. The quote is from p. 288.

89 *NZH*, 31 December 1883, p. 3.

90 Lady Barker, 'Christmas Day in New Zealand', in *A Christmas Cake in Four Quarters*, Macmillan, London, 1872, p. 277. The story also appears in D. M. Davin, ed., *New Zealand Short Stories*, Oxford University Press, Oxford, 1953. Barker may have been unaware that 'duff' was in fact a northern English term for pudding, deriving from 'dough'.

91 Enga Washbourn, *Courage and Camp Ovens: Five Generations at Golden Bay*, Reed, Wellington, 1970, p. 156.

92 Keith Sinclair, ed., *A Soldier's View of Empire: The Reminiscences of James Bodell 1831–92*, Bodley Head, London, 1982, pp. 135–6.

93 *Weekly News*, 19 December 1874, p. 5.

94 Jane Maria Atkinson to Emily E. Richmond, 27 December 1857, in Guy H. Scholefield, ed., *The Richmond-Atkinson Papers, Volume I*, Government Printer, Wellington, 1960, p. 331.

95 Jack Fowler to Martha Fowler, 1 January 1886 and 26 January 1887.

96 Charles Collier to Edward Collier, 7 January 1866, Collier family papers, MS-Papers-3946, ATL.

97 Jack Fowler to Martha Fowler, 5 October and 5 November 1884.

98 *NZS*, 26 December 1846, p. 3.

99 Sarah Amelia Courage, 'Lights and Shadows of Colonial Life: Twenty-six Years in Canterbury, New Zealand by a Settler's Wife', p. 73, qMS-0576, ATL.

100 *WI*, 1 January 1863, p. 3.

101 Charles Collier to Edward Collier, 7 January 1866; Drummond, *Auckland Journals of Vicesimus Lush*, p. 97 (writing of Christmas 1851).

102 *WCT*, 25 December 1867, p. 2.

103 *NZH*, 25 December 1893, p. 5.

104 *NZH*, 25 December 1875, p. 3; 25 December 1893, p. 5.

105 Drummond, *Thames Journals of Vicesimus Lush*, p. 144.

106 [Charles Rooking Carter], *Life and Recollections of a New Zealand Colonist*, Vol. II, the author, London, 1866, p. 10.

107 George Douch to his parents, 14 December 1877, printed in *Kent & Sussex Times*, 15 June 1878, p. 6, cited in Arnold, *Farthest Promised Land*, p. 303.

108 Helen M. Leach and Raelene Inglis, 'The Archaeology of Christmas Cakes', *Food and Foodways* 11 (2003), pp. 141–66.

109 *NZH*, 21 December 1866, p. 1; 24 December 1867, p. 1.

110 *NZH*, 23 December 1882, p. 4.

111 Drummond, *Auckland Journals of Vicesimus Lush*, p. 52.

112 Northcroft, *New Zealand Memories*, pp. 68–9.

113 Jean Boswell, *Dim Horizons*, Whitcombe & Tombs, Christchurch, 1955, p. 29.

114 *OW*, 24 December 1881, p. 21.

115 See Gibbons, 'Cultural Colonization', for a helpful discussion of this process.

116 *NZH*, 26 December 1881, p. 5.

117 *NZH*, 29 December 1879, p. 4.

118 *NZH*, 25 December 1879, p. 5; 25 December 1882, p. 5.

119 *NZH*, 25 December 1879, p. 5.

120 *OW*, 3 January 1863, p. 2.

121 *NZH*, 26 December 1876, p. 2.

122 Jack Fowler to Martha Fowler, 29 December 1886.

123 *NZH*, 3 January 1866, p. 5.

124 Hutton, *Stations of the Sun*, pp. 114–15.

125 Anna Dierks diary, translated by Theo Dierks, MS-Papers-2326, ATL. See, for example, her entries for 15 January 1877 and 31 December 1885.

126 Ellen Russell to Lucy Johnson, 1 January 1879, George Randall Johnson papers, folder 2, MS-Papers-0504, ATL.

127 *OW*, 9 January 1890, p. 20.

128 *NZH*, 23 December 1880, p. 4.

129 *NZH*, 28 December 1895, p. 5.

130 *OW*, 28 December 1872, p. 15.

131 Helen M. Thompson, *East of the Rock and Pillar: A History of the Strath Taieri and Macraes Districts*, Otago Centennial Historical Publications, Dunedin, 1949, p. 44; Jane Thomson, ed., *Southern People: A Dictionary of Otago Southland Biography*, Longacre / Dunedin City Council, Dunedin, 1998, p. 240.

132 *NZH*, 29 December 1888, supplement, p. 1.

133 *NZH*, 24 December 1873, p. 2.

134 *NZH*, 27 December 1872, p. 2.

135 *OW*, 2 January 1869, p. 14.

136 Sarah Marsden Smith diary, 25 December 1889, Misc-MS-1255, HC.

137 Esther C. Brown, *Scottish Mother*, Vantage, New York, 1957, p. 41.

138 Boswell, *Dim Horizons*, p. 29.

139 Anna Dierks diary, 31 December 1885.

140 Jack Fowler to Martha Fowler, 1 January 1886, 2 December 1886 and 11 November 1890.

141 Perry, *Eliza's Journal*, p. 168.

142 Hutton, *Stations of the Sun*, p. 117.

143 Hutton, *Stations of the Sun*, pp. 117–18; Golby and Purdue, *Making of the Modern Christmas*, pp. 71–5; see also Nissenbaum, *Battle for Christmas*, pp. 49–89.

144 *OW*, 26 December 1868, p. 16; 23 December 1876, p. 18; 15 December 1877, p. 19; 21 December

1878, Christmas supplement; 27 December 1879, Christmas supplement.

145 *NZH*, 25 December 1888, p. 5.

146 *NZT*, 26 December 1884, p. 16.

147 *The Imperial Readers (Southern Cross Series), First Reader*, Whitcombe & Tombs, Wellington, Christchurch and Dunedin, [1899], pp. 90–2.

148 *The Imperial Readers (Southern Cross Series), Third Reader*, Whitcombe & Tombs, Wellington, Christchurch and Dunedin, [1899], pp. 42–8.

149 Ellen Smith, 'Not a Poor Thing', p. 13.

150 William Forster Mills, Sudbury, Marton, to his mother in England, 31 December 1883, Mills letters, Anderson family papers, 91-302-1, ATL.

151 *NZH*, 1 January 1889, p. 6.

152 *New Zealand Times*, 14 December 1894, p. 3.

153 Helen B. Laurenson, *Going Up, Going Down: The Rise and Fall of the Department Store*, Auckland University Press, Auckland, 2005, pp. 100–1.

154 Kate McCosh Clark, *A Southern Cross Fairy Tale*, Sampson Low, Marston, Searle & Rivington, London, 1891.

155 Golby and Purdue, *Making of the Modern Christmas*, p. 76.

156 *NZH*, 28 December 1869, p. 4; 27 December 1872, p. 2.

157 Charles Collier to Edward Collier, 7 January 1866.

158 *NZS*, 22 December 1849, p. 2; 2 January 1850, p. 1.

159 Schmidt, *Consumer Rites*, pp. 5–11, 169–91.

CHAPTER TWO: NEW YEAR

1 *OW*, 9 January 1864, p. 8.

2 *OW*, 6 January 1865, p. 2.

3 *NZH*, 2 January 1874, p. 3.

4 *NZH*, 3 January 1881, p. 5.

5 *NZH*, 1 January 1879, p. 2.

6 Reminiscences of James McKerrow, 1899, p. 8, C069, OSM.

7 *OW*, 30 December 1887, p. 22.

8 Libby Hakaraia, *Matariki: The Maori New Year*, Reed, Auckland, 2004; Elsdon Best, *The Maori Division of Time*, Dominion Museum, Wellington, 1922.

9 Juliet Batten, leading light of a women's ritual group, has been a proponent of this and other seasonally appropriate adaptations of old festivals. See her book *Celebrating the Southern Seasons:*

Rituals for Aotearoa, rev. edn, Tandem Press, Auckland, 2005.

10 Hutton, *Stations of the Sun*, p. 2.

11 *New Zealand Gazette & Wellington Spectator*, 2 January 1841, p. 3.

12 *ST*, 4 January 1876, p. 2.

13 *OW*, 7 January 1882, p. 13.

14 Frederick Haslam to his mother, 22 December 1863–1 January 1864, Haslam family papers, MS-Papers-3895, Folder 4, ATL.

15 *OW*, 9 January 1864, p. 6.

16 *WH*, 2 January 1879, p. 2.

17 *NZH*, 10 January 1871, p. 3.

18 *NZH*, 1 January 1876, p. 3.

19 *TH*, 2 January 1895, p. 2.

20 'Auld Lang Syne', in Maurice Lindsay, ed., *The Burns Encyclopaedia*, Robert Hale, London, 1995 (full text available online at www.robertburns.org, accessed 30 January 2006).

21 James Kinsley, ed., *Robert Burns's Poems and Songs*, Everyman's Library, London, 1958, p. 316.

22 *NZH*, 6 January 1865, p. 5.

23 Alan St H. Brock, *A History of Fireworks*, Harrap, London, 1949, p. 158.

24 *Marlborough Express*, 2 January 1890, p. 2.

25 *OW*, 11 January 1879, p. 7.

26 *Star* (Christchurch), 2 January 1869, p. 2.

27 *NZH*, 1 January 1881, p. 5.

28 *NZH*, 3 January 1887, p. 4; 1 January 1896, p. 5.

29 *NZH*, 2 January 1879, p. 2.

30 *Star*, 2 January 1880, p. 3.

31 *OW*, 6 January 1883, p. 9.

32 *TH*, 2 January 1892, p. 2; *Star*, 2 January 1892, p. 3; *WCT*, 2 January 1895, p. 2.

33 *Inangahua Times*, 2 January 1896, p. 2.

34 *OW*, 9 January 1875, p. 16.

35 *Statistics of New Zealand*, 1891, p. 122; James Ng, *Windows on A Chinese Past*, Vol. 1, Otago Heritage Books, Dunedin, 1993, p. 180.

36 *NZH*, 31 December 1889, p. 5; 1 January 1890, p. 5.

37 *OW*, 4 January 1879, p. 16.

38 Thomas Burns diary, 1 January 1850, C-017, OSM.

39 *OW*, 11 January 1873, p. 13.

40 *OW*, 5 January 1878, p. 15.

41 *OW*, 5 January 1899, p. 25.

42 *Weekly News*, 3 January 1874, p. 12.

43 *OW*, 8 January 1881, p. 14.

44 *OW*, 7 January 1897, p. 16. Charges of drunkenness

feature largely in the early January court proceedings reported in most newspapers. For a good example, see the *Star*, 2 January 1879, p. 2.

45   *OW*, 7 January 1897, p. 43.
46   Sarah Marsden Smith diary, 31 December 1889.
47   William Turnbull Smith diary, 31 December 1863, MS-0578-A, HC.
48   *Star*, 3 January 1870, p. 2.
49   McNeill, *Silver Bough*, pp. 104–8; Hutton, *Stations of the Sun*, pp. 50–2; Miles, *Christmas Customs*, pp. 323–6.
50   Charles Hayward diary, 1 January 1866. 'Robt' may have been Hayward's brother-in-law, Robert Lees.
51   *NZP*, 2 January 1893, p. 130.
52   *WI*, 3 January 1874, p. 3.
53   *OW*, 7 January 1882, p. 13.
54   *OW*, 7 January 1897, p. 17.
55   *WT*, 2 January 1875, p. 2.
56   *OW*, 4 January 1879, p. 16.
57   'Larrikin', in *Oxford English Dictionary*, online at www.oed.com (accessed 16 January 2006).
58   *NZH*, 1 January 1874, p. 3.
59   *NZH*, 1 January 1881, p. 5; *WT*, 3 January 1882, p. 2.
60   *NZH*, 2 January 1877, p. 3.
61   *TH*, 2 January 1890, p. 2.
62   *NZH*, 4 January 1888, p. 4.
63   Quote from *TH*, 2 January 1895, p. 2.
64   *WH*, 2 January 1879, p. 2.
65   *OW*, 12 January 1899, p. 26.
66   *OW*, 12 January 1884, p. 13.
67   *Mataura Ensign*, 4 January 1898, p. 2.
68   Erik Olssen, *A History of Otago*, McIndoe, Dunedin, 1984, pp. 92–5. On colonial childhood, see Belich, *Paradise Reforged*, pp. 356–67.
69   Horton Davies, *Worship and Theology in England From Watts and Wesley to Martineau, 1690–1900*, Eerdmans, Grand Rapids, Michigan, 1996, Part 1, pp. 191–2 and 197–200; and Part 2, pp. 260–4; Schmidt, *Consumer Rites*, pp. 119–21.
70   S. J. D. Green, *Religion in the Age of Decline: Organisation and Experience in Industrial Yorkshire 1870–1920*, Cambridge University Press, Cambridge, 1996, pp. 339–40; John Wolffe, *God and Greater Britain: Religion and National Life in Britain and Ireland 1843–1945*, Routledge, London, 1994, pp. 75, 84–5; S. C. Williams, *Religious Belief and Popular Culture in Southwark c.1880–1939*, Oxford University Press, Oxford, 1999, pp. 92–5; and

Jeffrey Cox, *The English Churches in a Secular Society: Lambeth, 1870–1930*, Oxford University Press, New York, 1982, pp. 102–3.
71   *WI*, 2 January 1869, p. 3.
72   *OW*, 9 January 1875, p. 15.
73   *Star*, 2 January 1873, p. 2.
74   *TH*, 2 January 1885, p. 2.
75   *Rules and Regulations of the Methodist Church of New Zealand*, Christchurch, 1916, p. 14. These regulations for the recently united church – previously made up of the separate Wesleyan, Primitive Methodist, Bible Christian and Free Methodist churches – reflected long-standing practice in these churches.
76   Thomas Ferens diary, 31 December 1848, C-039; Thomas Ferens diary, 31 December 1868 and 31 December 1869, Thomas Ferens papers, AG-99, Box 2, OSM.
77   *NEM*, 3 January 1899, p. 2.
78   *NZH*, 1 January 1880, p. 5.
79   *NZH*, 1 January 1878, p. 2.
80   *OW*, 10 January 1874, p. 1; for an example of evergreens see *OW*, 8 January 1881, p. 22.
81   Mary Taylor diary, 31 December 1858, Mary Catherine Medley (née Taylor) papers, MS-Papers-3762, Folder 1, ATL.
82   *WT*, 2 January 1886, p. 2.
83   John Christie diary, undated note (probably New Year 1878), AG-102 1-1, OSM.
84   William Muir diary, 31 December 1863, SA-008, OSM.
85   Walter Riddell diary, 1 January 1866, C-090, OSM.
86   Walter Riddell diary, 3 January 1869.
87   Jim McAloon, *No Idle Rich: The Wealthy in Canterbury and Otago 1840–1914*, Otago University Press, Dunedin, 2002, p. 173.
88   *OW*, 3 January 1857, p. 3.
89   *NZH*, 31 December 1864, p. 3.
90   Schmidt, *Consumer Rites*, p. 118.
91   Mary Taylor diary, 31 December 1859.
92   Donald McLean diary, 1 January 1859, MS-1222, ATL.
93   Robert Nicol to George Nicol, 28 January 1878, MS-Papers-4083, ATL.
94   *OW*, 9 January 1896, p. 14.
95   George Hepburn to Thomas Martin, 4 January 1861.
96   *WI*, 4 January 1861, p. 3.

97   *Star*, 3 January 1899, p. 2. The holiday was on 2 January that year as New Year's Day fell on a Sunday.

98   Edward Fletcher Roberts diary, 1 January 1898, MS-0485, HC.

99   *WI*, 10 January 1862, p. 3.

100 *OW*, 6 January 1883, p. 13.

101 Two important studies of the friendly societies in New Zealand make only brief mention of their convivial aspects: see Jennifer Carlyon, 'Friendly Societies 1842–1939', *NZJH* 32, 2 (1998), pp. 121–42; and David Thomson, *A World Without Welfare: New Zealand's Colonial Experiment*, Auckland University Press, Auckland, 1998, pp. 35–51. Erik Olssen, however, notes the significance of conviviality, and of public displays, for the friendly societies: see his essay 'Friendly Societies in New Zealand, 1840–1990', in Marcel van der Linden, ed., *Social Security Mutualism: The Comparative History of Mutual Benefit Societies*, Lang, Berne, 1996, pp. 177–206. Studies of English friendly societies show that the convivial aspects of these groups were essential in attracting members: see P. H. J. H. Gosden, *The Friendly Societies in England 1815–1875*, University of Manchester Press, Manchester, 1960, pp. 115–37.

102 For examples of reports of this annual event see *WI*, 2 January 1856, p. 3; 2 January 1858, p. 3.

103 *WI*, 26 December 1857, p. 2; 2 January 1858, p. 3.

104 David Keen, 'Feeding the Lambs: The Influence of Sunday Schools on the Socialization of Children in Otago and Southland, 1848–1901', PhD thesis, University of Otago, 1999, pp. 136–139, 144–6, 151.

105 Frederick Haslam to his mother, 22 December 1863–1 January 1864.

106 *Star*, 1 January 1869, p. 2.

107 *NZH*, 3 January 1887, p. 6.

108 *WCT*, 2 January 1895, p. 2.

109 Alexander Don, *Memories of the Golden Road: A History of the Presbyterian Church in Central Otago*, Reed, Dunedin, [1936], p. 432.

110 *OW*, 7 January 1897, p. 25.

111 *OW*, 7 January 1871, p. 14.

112 *NZH*, 5 January 1870, p. 4.

113 *Star*, 2 January 1889, p. 3.

114 Ibid.

115 David Mackie, '1948 tapes' (tapes of local pioneers recorded by unidentified members of the New Zealand Army in 1948), Lakes District Museum, Arrowtown.

116 *NZH*, 7 January 1873, p. 3.

117 *NZH*, 9 January 1865, p. 5; 10 January 1866, p. 5; *WI*, 9 January 1864, p. 6.

118 *OW*, 9 January 1864, p. 4.

119 *Auckland Weekly News*, 6 January 1899, supplement, p. 1.

120 For examples of this long-standing annual event, see *Star*, 1 January 1869, p. 2; 2 January 1875, p. 2; 2 January 1879, p. 3; 2 January 1885, p. 4; 2 January 1895, p. 2.

121 *OW*, 9 January 1864, p. 4.

122 G. J. Griffiths, 'Jones, Shadrach Edward Robert', in *DNZB, Vol. One, 1769–1869*, Allen & Unwin / Department of Internal Affairs, Wellington, 1990, pp. 213–4; and Robert Valpy Fulton, *Medical Practice in Otago and Southland in the Early Days*, Otago Daily Times, Dunedin, 1922, pp. 198–204.

123 *OW*, 28 December 1861, p. 5; 4 January 1862, p. 5.

124 'James Strachan's Experiences: My First Twelve Years on my Own – Commencing from 20th April, 1856 – nearly 61 years ago', MS-0563, HC.

125 Irvine Roxburgh, *Wanaka Story: A History of the Wanaka, Hawea, Tarras and Surrounding Districts*, Otago Centennial Historical Publications, Dunedin, 1957, p. 102.

126 John Wilson, *Reminiscences of the Early Settlement of Dunedin and South Otago*, Wilkie, Dunedin, 1912, pp. 184–5.

127 James Marchbanks, reminiscences, MS-0550, HC.

128 *OW*, 14 January 1882, p. 13.

129 *OW*, 5 January 1867, p. 9. The newspaper reports always gave attendance numbers. For a summary, see Shiobhan O'Donnell, 'Dancing at the Auld Cale: A History of Highland Dancing in Dunedin between 1863 and 1900', BA Hons dissertation, University of Otago, 1998, pp. 26–7.

130 This list is compiled from reports in the *OW*. On the South Otago games and 'competitive circuit', see also Jennifer Coleman, 'Transmigration of the Piob Mhor: The Scottish Highland Piping Tradition in the South Island of New Zealand, with Particular Reference to Southland, Otago and South Canterbury, to 1940', PhD thesis, University of Otago, 1996, pp. 195–8. For evidence of pipers competing in several different games in the same region, see the lists in Coleman's appendices.

131 *ST*, 4 January 1876, p. 2.

132 Donald McLean diary, 25 December 1848.

133 *NZS*, 2 January 1850, p. 2; 4 January 1851, p. 2; 3 January 1852, p. 3; *WI*, 2 January 1866, p. 5.

134 *NZH*, 1 January 1869, p. 3; 2 January 1869, p. 5.

135 *Star*, 3 January 1882, p. 3.

136 *WI*, 12 January 1864, p. 3; Maureen Molloy, *Those Who Speak to the Heart: The Nova Scotian Scots at Waipu 1854–1920*, Dunmore, Palmerston North, 1991, p. 58.

137 Tom Brooking, 'Sharing out the Haggis: The Special Scottish Contribution to New Zealand History', in Tom Brooking and Jennie Coleman, eds, *The Heather and the Fern: Scottish Migration and New Zealand Settlement*, Otago University Press, Dunedin, 2003, p. 49.

138 Peter Womack, *Improvement and Romance: Constructing the Myth of the Highlands*, Macmillan, Basingstoke, 1989, p. 145. On Caledonia and Roman Britain, see also Norman Davies, *The Isles: A History*, Macmillan, London, 1999, pp. 105–50.

139 Womack, *Improvement and Romance*; T. M. Devine, *The Scottish Nation: A History 1700–2000*, Viking, Harmondsworth, 1999, pp. 231–45; Murray G. H. Pittock, *The Invention of Scotland: The Stuart Myth and the Scottish Identity, 1638 to the Present*, Routledge, London, 1991; and Hugh Trevor-Roper, 'The Invention of Tradition: The Highland Tradition of Scotland', in Eric Hobsbawm and Terence Ranger, eds., *The Invention of Tradition*, Cambridge University Press, Cambridge, 1992, pp. 15–41.

140 Eric Richards, 'Australia and the Scottish Connection, 1788–1914', in R. A. Cage, ed., *The Scots Abroad: Labour, Capital Enterprise, 1750–1914*, Croom Helm, London, 1985, pp. 141–2.

141 Caledonian Society of Otago Directors' Minute Book, 21 February 1868 and 6 March 1868, MS-1045/001, HC. These plans were for a special Caledonian gathering to be held during the Duke of Edinburgh's visit to Otago, which was delayed until the following year.

142 *Star*, 3 January 1899, p. 2; *ODT*, 4 January 1886, p. 3.

143 *ODT*, 3 January 1880, cited in O'Donnell, 'History of Highland Dancing', pp. 27–9, in a discussion of the popularity of athletic over cultural events. Jennie Coleman also suggests that 'Highland piping and dancing formed but a colourful contributing element to the predominantly athletic activities of the gatherings': see 'Transmigration of the Piob Mhor', pp. 481–2.

144 *OW*, 10 January 1874, p. 6.

145 Twenty-Third Annual Report and Balance Sheet of the Caledonian Society of Otago, 26 October 1885, inserted in Caledonian Society of Otago, Directors' Minute Book 1885–1898, MS-1045/007, HC. While no first name or initial is given for the member Sew Hoy, it seems most likely to have been merchant Choie Sew Hoy, 'the greatest Chinese in 19th century Otago'. See James Ng's entry on the Sew Hoys in Thomson, *Southern People*, pp. 449–50.

146 *WI*, 2 January 1866, p. 5; 3 January 1867, p. 3; 2 January 1869, p. 3.

147 See, for example, a New Year report from Edinburgh: 'As usual again, alas, throughout the day, the streets were thronged with reeling, ranting drunkards – many of them mere boys' (*OW*, 26 March 1864, p. 1). See also W. W. Knox, *Industrial Nation: Work, Culture and Society in Scotland, 1800–Present*, Edinburgh University Press, Edinburgh, 1999, p. 94.

148 Alison Clarke, 'A Godly Rhythm: Keeping the Sabbath in Otago, 1870–1890', in John Stenhouse and Jane Thomson, eds, *Building God's Own Country: Historical Essays on Religions in New Zealand*, Otago University Press, Dunedin, 2004, pp. 46–59; H. R. Jackson, *Churches and People in Australia and New Zealand 1860–1930*, Allen & Unwin, Wellington, 1987, pp. 104–24.

149 *OW*, 6 January 1888, p. 11.

150 *WT*, 3 January 1882, p. 2.

151 *Star*, 2 January 1883, p. 3.

152 *NZH*, 3 January 1873, p. 4.

153 *ST*, 3 January 1878, p. 3.

154 'Our Home Letter', *NZH*, 30 December 1886, p. 9.

THREE: EASTER

1 Hutton, *Stations of the Sun*, pp. 151–78.

2 *OW*, 10 October 1874, p. 10.

3 'A Lenten Address', 1898, Hocken Pamphlets, Volume 172, Number 26, HC.

4 *NZT*, 11 April 1884, p. 15.

5 *NZH*, 10 April 1895, p. 7.

6 *OW*, 3 April 1890, p. 32.

7 Drummond, *Auckland Journals of Vicesimus Lush*, p. 72.

8   Drummond, *Thames Journals of Vicesimus Lush*, p. 195.
9   Ibid., p. 53.
10 Caroline Abraham to Sophia Marriott, [20 March 1857?], MS-Papers-2305, ATL. Charles Abraham later became Anglican Bishop of Wellington.
11 St Mary's Parish Magazine, March 1897, St Mary's Anglican Church, Mornington, records, MS-1098/004, HC.
12 St Mary's Parish Magazine, May 1897, May 1896, April 1897.
13 *NZH*, 1 April 1893, supplement, p. 1.
14 I checked the dates of 276 nineteenth-century marriages in the transcripts of registers from: St Matthew's Anglican Church, Dunedin; St John's Anglican Church, Invercargill; and St Paul's Anglican Church (later the Cathedral), Dunedin (these transcripts, made by members of the New Zealand Society of Genealogists, are held in the HC and other local research libraries). Of these, 41, or 14.9 per cent, took place in Lent or Holy Week, while the 46-day period of Lent and Holy Week makes up 12.6 per cent of the year. Four of the 41 marriages took place in Holy Week.
15 I checked the dates of 271 nineteenth-century marriages in the index to Roman Catholic marriages in the Diocese of Dunedin (as above, compiled by members of the New Zealand Society of Genealogists and held in the HC and other local research libraries). Ten marriages – just 3.7% – took place during Lent and Holy Week, and only one of those was in Holy Week. The sample included seven Shrove Tuesday marriages.
16 Danaher, *Year in Ireland*, pp. 43–6.
17 *OW*, 13 March 1875, p. 17.
18 Letter to the editor from Wm Minchin, *WI*, 31 March 1864, p. 3.
19 These ceremonies generally received detailed coverage in the *NZT*.
20 Jessie Mackay to Jane Lamb, 16 April 1873, Lamb papers, Biog Box 70-14, OSM.
21 *NZH*, 19 April 1886, p. 5.
22 *NZT*, 16 March 1894, p. 6.
23 *NZT*, 6 April 1888, pp. 17–18.
24 *NZT*, 23 April 1897, p. 18.
25 *NZH*, 4 April 1896, p. 5.
26 *NZH*, 12 April 1884, p. 5. Jervois, son of the governor, appears to have been a visitor to Auckland.
27 *Timaru Herald*, 18 April 1892, p. 2.
28 *Outlook*, 8 April 1899, p. 3. See also *NZP*, 1 November 1888, p. 86.
29 *Proceedings of the General Assembly of the Presbyterian Church of New Zealand 1931*, Otago Daily Times, Dunedin, 1931, pp. 25, 207. The *Outlook* approved this move: see 15 June 1931, p. 7.
30 Thomas Ferens diary, 21 and 23 April 1848, C039, OSM. Easter goes unremarked in Ferens's diary for 1869.
31 James Watkin diary, 6 April 1844, MS-0440/04, HC.
32 *New Zealand Wesleyan*, 1 August 1874, p. 134.
33 *ODT*, 25 March 1864, p. 4.
34 George Sumpter diary, 18 April 1862, C106, OSM.
35 Frederic Charles Otto diary transcript, 17 April 1870, Misc-MS-1113, HC.
36 Charlotte Godley to Sarah Wynne, March 1850, in Godley, *Letters from Early New Zealand*, pp. 18–19.
37 *OW*, 19 March 1853, p. 2. The fair was delayed for a week.
38 James Kilgour to his brother, 30 April 1867, BB33, OSM.
39 Jack Fowler to Martha Fowler, 18 April 1888, 16 April 1890.
40 *WI*, 15 April 1865, p. 3.
41 Drummond, *Thames Journals of Vicesimus Lush*, p. 133.
42 *ODT*, 11 April 1885, supplement, p. 2.
43 P. J. Lineham, 'Freethinkers in Nineteenth-Century New Zealand', *NZJH* 19, 1 (1985), p. 69. See also Peter J. Lineham, 'Christian Reaction to Freethought and Rationalism in New Zealand', *Journal of Religious History* 15 (1988), pp. 236–50.
44 *NZH*, 31 March 1877, p. 2, and 20 April 1878, p. 2; *TH*, 26 April 1886, p. 2.
45 *ODT*, 6 April 1882, p. 3.
46 *NZT*, 8 April 1887, p. 16.
47 *NZH*, 3 April 1879, p. 5; 7 April 1879, p. 6; 8 April 1879, p. 6.
48 *NZH*, 27 March 1880, p. 4. It was unclear who had mistakenly publicised the occasion without proper confirmation – suspicion fell on the ferry company manager who gained profits from carrying the excursionists to Orakei, but he was cleared of responsibility.
49 *OW*, 23 March 1899, p. 34; 30 March 1899, p. 34.
50 Catherine Squires (née Dewe) diary, 6 and 8 April 1860, 30 March 1861, 6 and 7 April 1861, M-61 and

M-62, OSM. Catherine's father, John Dewe, was later an ordained Anglican priest.

51 Bosco Peters, *The Anglican Eucharist in New Zealand 1814–1989*, Grove, Bramcote, Nottingham, 1992, p. 14.

52 Arnold Hunt, 'The Lord's Supper in Early Modern England', *Past and Present* 161 (1998), pp. 82–3.

53 Frances Knight, *The Nineteenth-Century Church and English Society*, Cambridge University Press, Cambridge, 1995, pp. 53–4.

54 St Mark's Anglican Church, Balclutha, Service Register 1876–1882, AG-519/022; St Peters Anglican Church, Queenstown, Service Register 1881–1891, AG-166/018, HC.

55 George Sumpter diary, 5 October 1862.

56 *NZH*, 1 April 1872, p. 2.

57 *Weekly News*, 11 April 1874, p. 6.

58 *NZH*, 20 April 1897, p. 4.

59 *NZH*, 18 April 1881, p. 5.

60 *HBH*, 6 April 1896, p. 2.

61 *Poverty Bay Herald*, 8 April 1890, p. 2.

62 Ibid.

63 *NZT*, 14 April 1893, p. 20.

64 *NZT*, 7 April 1893, p. 17.

65 *NZT*, 15 April 1887, p. 16; 18 April 1884, pp. 17–18.

66 S. J. Connolly, *Priests and People in Pre-Famine Ireland 1780–1845*, Gill & Macmillan, Dublin, 1982; Emmet Larkin, 'The Devotional Revolution in Ireland, 1850–75', *American Historical Review* 77 (1972), pp. 625–52.

67 Michael King, *God's Farthest Outpost: A History of Catholics in New Zealand*, Penguin, Auckland, 1997, pp. 111–12; Jackson, *Churches & People*, pp. 65–76, 119–24.

68 Helen Mills to her mother, 4 April 1885, Mills letters.

69 Emily Cumming Harris diary, 23 April 1886, MS-Papers-1284, ATL.

70 Tanya Gulevich, *Encyclopedia of Easter, Carnival and Lent*, Omnigraphics, Detroit, 2002, pp. 355–60. The highly scented white *Lilium longiflorum* could be forced to bloom early, and by the turn of the century it had become popular as an Easter decoration. Known as the Easter lily in North America and Europe, this is the same variety now popular as the Christmas lily in Australasia – a reminder of the differences between celebrations in the two hemispheres.

71 *NZH*, 3 April 1893, p. 3.

72 *NZH*, 13 April 1887, p. 4; 18 April 1892, p. 6.

73 Gibbons, 'Cultural Colonization'.

74 *Star*, 17 April 1876, p. 2.

75 *NZH*, 11 April 1890, p. 6.

76 *NEM*, 29 March 1880, p. 2.

77 Alison Clarke, 'Communities Celebrating Landscapes: Harvest Festivities in Nineteenth-Century Otago', in Tony Ballantyne and Judith A. Bennett, eds *Landscape/Community: Perspectives from New Zealand History*, Otago University Press, Dunedin, 2005, pp. 103–16.

78 *NZH*, 4 April 1890, p. 5.

79 *NEM*, 7 April 1890, p. 2.

80 *OW*, 18 April 1895, p. 18.

81 Anna Dierks diary, 12 April 1875.

82 Schmidt, *Consumer Rites*, pp. 199–201.

83 *NZH*, 20 April 1897, p. 6.

84 *Marlborough Express*, 7 April 1885, p. 2.

85 Schmidt, *Consumer Rites*, pp. 210–19; Hutton, *Stations of the Sun*, p. 204.

86 *Evening Post*, 22 March 1910, p. 9.

87 Hutton, *Stations of the Sun*, pp. 198–203; Elizabeth Pleck, *Celebrating the Family: Ethnicity, Consumer Culture, and Family Rituals*, Harvard University Press, Cambridge, Massachusetts, 2000, pp. 78–80; Venetia Newall, *An Egg at Easter*, Routledge, London, 1971.

88 *NZH*, 24 March 1894, p. 4.

89 *NZT*, 16 April 1897, p. 11.

90 Drummond, *Auckland Journals of Vicesimus Lush*, p. 74.

91 *Northern Advocate* (Whangerei), 9 April 1887, p. 2; *ST*, 6 April 1882, p. 3.

92 Boswell, *Dim Horizons*, p. 127.

93 *NZH*, 7 April 1898, p. 5.

94 *HBH*, 7 April 1890, p. 2.

95 *Mt Ida Chronicle*, 27 March 1880, p. 2.

96 Hutton, *Stations of the Sun*, pp. 192–3; Alan Davidson, *The Oxford Companion to Food*, Oxford University Press, Oxford, 1999, p. 114.

97 *NZH*, 30 March 1877, p. 2.

98 *NZH*, 7 April 1898, p. 5.

99 *NZH*, 19 April 1881, p. 4.

100 Hutton, *Stations of the Sun*, p. 204.

101 Danaher, *Year in Ireland*, pp. 82–3.

102 Charlotte Godley to Sarah Wynne, March–May 1852, in Godley, *Letters from Early New Zealand*,

p. 309.

103 *NZS*, 14 April 1852, p. 3.

104 *NZH*, 23 April 1867, p. 3; 11 April 1882, p. 4.

105 *OW*, 27 April 1866, p. 16.

106 *Star*, 11 April 1871, p. 3; *Feilding Star*, 4 April 1899, p. 2.

107 *OW*, 6 April 1899, p. 28.

108 *North Otago Times*, 4 April 1899, p. 2.

109 *OW*, 22 April 1897, p. 25.

110 *NEM*, 3 April 1890, p. 2.

111 *OW*, 19 April 1879, p. 11. See also *OW*, 16 April 1896, p. 28.

112 Jock Phillips, *A Man's Country? The Image of the Pakeha Male: A History*, revised edn, Penguin, Auckland, 1996, pp. 33–4; Arnold, *Farthest Promised Land*, pp. 29–30, 246.

113 Letter from Joseph Brocklesby, 24 April 1875, printed in *Labourer* (Boston), 24 July 1875, cited in Arnold, *Farthest Promised Land*, p. 285.

114 Letter from John Gregory, May 1873, printed in *Labourers' Union Chronicle*, 6 December 1873, cited in Arnold, *Farthest Promised Land*, p. 246.

115 John Crawford, 'Volunteer Force', in Ian McGibbon, ed., *The Oxford Companion to New Zealand Military History*, Oxford University Press, Auckland, 2000, pp. 566–71; Peter Cooke, *Defending New Zealand: Ramparts on the Sea 1840s–1950s*, Defence of New Zealand Study Group, Wellington, 2000, pp. 135–78.

116 For example, see the report of the encampment on Auckland's North Shore, *NZH*, 8 April 1898, p. 5.

117 *OW*, 7 April 1877, p. 17.

118 *Wanganui Chronicle*, 16 April 1895, p. 2; *OW*, 18 April 1895, p. 22.

119 William Brooks diary, 28 March 1880, MS-0461,

HC.

120 *WT*, 16 April 1881, p. 2; 20 April 1881 (a special edition reporting on the encampment), *NZH*, 19 April 1881, p. 5.

121 *OW*, 19 April 1873, p. 15.

CONCLUSION: THE EVOLUTION OF THE
NEW ZEALAND HOLIDAY

1   *OW*, 6 January 1872, p. 1.

2   Ibid.

3   *OW*, 9 January 1886, p. 12.

4   Jack Fowler to Martha Fowler, 26 January 1887.

5   Jack Fowler to Martha Fowler, 18 April 1888.

6   *TH*, 19 April 1876, p. 2.

7   Jack Fowler to Martha Fowler, 3 January 1884; 29 December 1884.

8   Fairburn, *Ideal Society and its Enemies*. See *NZJH* 25, 2 (1991), for various responses to Fairburn.

9   Sarah Derry to Pollie Derry, postmarked 22 February 1875, Derry family letters, MS-Papers-1043, ATL.

10 Gibbons, 'Cultural Colonization'; Peter Gibbons, 'Non-fiction', in Terry Sturm, ed., *The Oxford History of New Zealand Literature*, 2nd edn, Oxford University Press, Auckland, 1998, pp. 31–118.

11 On Diwali and its adaptation to the New Zealand context, see Henry Johnson and Guil Figgins, 'Diwali Downunder: Transforming and Performing Indian Tradition in Aotearoa/New Zealand', *New Zealand Journal of Media Studies*, 9, 1 (2005), www.nzetc.org/tm/scholarly/tei-Sch091JMS-t1-g1-t5.html.

· ✒

Armstrong, Neil, 'Christmas in Nineteenth-Century Britain and America: A Historiographical Overview', *Cultural and Social History* 1 (2004), pp. 118–25.

Arnold, Rollo, *The Farthest Promised Land: English Villagers, New Zealand Immigrants of the 1870s*, Victoria University Press, Wellington, 1981.

Batten, Juliet, *Celebrating the Southern Seasons: Rituals for Aotearoa*, rev. edn, Tandem Press, Auckland, 2005.

Best, Elsdon, *The Maori Division of Time*, Dominion Museum, Wellington, 1922.

Brooking, Tom, and Jennie Coleman, eds., *The Heather and the Fern: Scottish Migration and New Zealand Settlement*, Otago University Press, Dunedin, 2003.

Buchanan, Robert H., 'Calendar Customs: Part 1. New Year's Day to Michaelmas', *Ulster Folklife* 8 (1962), pp. 15–34.

_____, 'Calendar Customs: Part 2. Harvest to Christmas', *Ulster Folklife* 9 (1963), pp. 61–79.

Clarke, Alison, 'Communities Celebrating Landscapes: Harvest Festivities in Nineteenth-Century Otago', in Tony Ballantyne and Judith A. Bennett, eds, *Landscape/Community: Perspectives from New Zealand History*, Otago University Press, Dunedin, 2005, pp. 103–16.

_____, '"Days of Heaven on Earth": Presbyterian Communion Seasons in Nineteenth-Century Otago', *Journal of Religious History* 26 (2002), pp. 274–97.

_____, '"With one accord rejoice on this glad day": Celebrating the Monarchy in Nineteenth-Century Otago', *New Zealand Journal of History* 36, 2 (2002), pp. 137–60.

Connelly, Mark, *Christmas: A Social History*, Tauris, London, 1999.

Danaher, Kevin, *The Year in Ireland: Irish Calendar Customs*, Irish Books & Media, Minneapolis, 1972.

Davidson, Allan K., *Christianity in Aotearoa: A History of Church and Society in New Zealand*, 3rd edn, Education for Ministry, Wellington, 2004.

Fraser, Lyndon, ed., *A Distant Shore: Irish Migration and New Zealand Settlement*, Otago University Press, Dunedin, 2000.

Golby, J. M., and A. W. Purdue, *The Making of the Modern Christmas*, rev. edn, Sutton, Stroud, Gloucestershire, 2000.

Gibbons, Peter, 'Cultural Colonization and National Identity', *New Zealand Journal of History* 36, 1 (2002), pp. 5–17.

Hakaraia, Libby, *Matariki: The Maori New Year*, Reed, Auckland, 2004.

Hutton, Ronald, *The Stations of the Sun: A History of the Ritual Year in Britain*, Oxford University Press, Oxford, 1996.

Jackson, Hugh, *Churches and People in Australia and New Zealand 1860–1930*, Allen & Unwin, Wellington, 1987.

Jarvie, Grant, *Highland Games: The Making of the Myth*, Edinburgh University Press, Edinburgh, 1991.

Keyte, Hugh, and Andrew Parrott, eds, *The New Oxford Book of Carols*, Oxford University Press, Oxford, 1992.

Leach, Helen M., and Raelene Inglis, 'The Archaeology of Christmas Cakes', *Food and Foodways* 11 (2003), pp. 141–66.

McNeill, F. Marian, *The Silver Bough, Volumes Two and Three: A Calendar of Scottish National Festivals*, Maclellan, Glasgow, 1961.

Maddock, Shirley, and Michael Easther, *A Christmas Garland: A New Zealand Christmas Album 1642–1900 in Twelve Parts*, Collins, Auckland, 1980.

Miles, Clement A., *Christmas Customs and Traditions: Their History and Significance*. Dover, New York, 1976 (first published 1912).

Mitchell, Isabella, 'Picnics in New Zealand during the Late Nineteenth and Early Twentieth Centuries: An Interpretive Study', MA thesis, Massey University, Palmerston North, 1995.

Newall, Venetia, *An Egg at Easter: A Folklore Study*, Routledge, London, 1971.

Nissenbaum, Stephen, *The Battle for Christmas*, Vintage, New York, 1996.

Patterson, Brad, ed., *The Irish in New Zealand: Historical Contexts and Perspectives*, Stout Research Centre, Wellington, 2002.

_____, *Ulster–New Zealand Migration and Cultural Transfers*, Four Courts, Dublin, 2006.

Russell, Alice, *Bank Holidays: A Victorian Invention and Modern Institution*, Minerva, London, 2000.

Schmidt, Leigh Eric, *Consumer Rites: The Buying and Selling of American Holidays*, Princeton University Press, Princeton, 1995.

Stapleton, Maisy, and Patricia McDonald, *Christmas in the Colonies*, Ell, Sydney, 1981.

Workers' Holidays in New Zealand: A Brief History, Trade Union History Project, Wellington, 1997.

Zerubavel, Eviatar, *Hidden Rhythms: Schedules and Calendars in Social Life*, University of Chicago Press, Chicago, 1981.